Editors
Gillian Eve Makepeace, M.S.
Sara Connolly

Illustrator
Clint McKnight

Cover Artist
Brenda DiAntonis

Editor In Chief
Ina Massler Levin, M.A.

Creative Director
Karen J. Goldfluss, M.S. Ed.

Art Production Manager
Kevin Barnes

Art Coordinator
Renée Christine Yates

Imaging
Nathan P. Rivera
Ariyanna Simien

Publisher
Mary D. Smith, M.S. Ed.

MEDIA LITERACY

Grade 5

Includes Standards

- Acquire tools to become media literate
- Learn about a variety of forms of media
- Interpret the true messages in media

Buy Cheesy Bits! They're delicious!

Author

Melissa Hart, M.F.A.

Teacher Created Resources, Inc.
6421 Industry Way
Westminster, CA 92683
www.teachercreated.com

ISBN: 978-1-4206-2778-7

© 2008 Teacher Created Resources, Inc.
Made in U.S.A.

Table of Contents

Table of Contents *(cont.)*

Foreword

At its core, this book teaches children and young people how to think critically about media messages, particularly visual media messages.

As the author points out, we are subjected to thousands of mediated images each day. They flash by us so fast that we have no time to think about them. Indeed most are designed to by-pass critical thought. They are carefully crafted to be felt. They tap into our emotions—fear, insecurity, sentimentality, prejudices. Often they purport to portray reality so that, with time, we unquestioningly treat them as being true, and we shape our behavior accordingly, divorced from the world around us.

Nowhere in our formal education have we been taught how to assess and critique these messages and so we have been buffeted by their impact, whether in the purchase of unneeded products, in how we perceive our abilities, or in the way we vote on Election Day. Media education, on the other hand, helps students become smarter in all aspects of their lives.

This book, with its fascinating and fun exercises, is intended to prepare children, a new generation, to see—literally—media images differently, critically. Once given the tools to analyze and think about what they see, children are astonishingly perceptive.

Students are shown how to put their newly acquired skills and insights to use. The skills learned here (and as presented, they are fun to learn) will carry over into other disciplines. Critical thinking about media statistics connects with math. Realizing the role of media-caused anxiety tells us much about psychology and even politics. Analyzing how stories are compellingly told on the screen teaches about clear, vivid writing. The list goes on and on.

More than learning how to make thoughtful, informed decisions and to shape a new, questioning relationship with media, young people also learn how to transform their lives. They perceive themselves differently and more positively. They soon learn that media literacy skills can be applied to all aspects of life.

Young people are great teachers. The great hope is that they will share their new knowledge with their parents and other adults so that, as a society, we all will become more aware and media literate.

Over the years, the media, which have such great potential to perform good, have done greater and greater harm. We have seen an exponential growth in irresponsible content—more violence, more commercialism, more sexualization, more fear-mongering and more deception. Public service has become a rarity. The one sure way to reverse the trend is for audiences to become media literate—for them to recognize the personal and societal consequences of irresponsible media messages and media consumption.

If audiences find such messages unfit for consumption and reject them, media decision-makers must change the media. Indeed, a media-literate public, armed with the tools taught in this text and elsewhere, has the power to force media to redeem themselves and fulfill their great potential and promise.

—*Rick Seifert and Rebecca Woolington*
MediaThink

How to Use This Book

Media surrounds us, from the moment we wake up in the morning until we go to bed at night. *Media Literacy, Grade 5* gives students the opportunity to study most forms of media to which they are exposed almost every day. Each assignment conforms to one or more of the McRel standards for grade 5, as noted on pages 6 and 7.

The book begins with a general discussion of media literacy, of the various forms of media and how consumers are exposed to it. Students are asked to chart their own media consumption, and to examine several forms of media for healthy and unhealthy messages including propaganda and stereotypes.

Historical overviews of each genre in media preface each section of the book. These descriptions allow students to understand how a particular genre has changed over time, or has given way to a new form of media. Photographs from the National Archives and the Library of Congress offer students the opportunity to view and analyze examples of media from the past and compare them to contemporary media.

Image courtesy of the Library of Congress, Prints and Photographs Division (LC-USZ62-2589)

In each section of the book, students are asked to deconstruct media in a variety of ways, through multiple choice questions, matching exercises, compositions, reviews, and charts. Many assignments require research with the use of books, encyclopedias, and/or the Internet. Each section concludes by offering students the opportunity to create a tangible example of the media genre they have studied. These hands-on projects can be completed alone or in small groups. They offer numerous opportunities for group discussion, and for demonstration among students and for parents.

A final project allows students to choose a favorite form of media and create an example. Later, they are asked to deconstruct what they have created to demonstrate a working knowledge of media literacy. A certificate on page 131 of the book can be reproduced and passed out to students as an acknowledgement of completing this book.

The final page offers you, the teacher, additional resources for the study of media literacy, including websites, organizations, and books. We hope that *Media Literacy, Grade 5* will become a valuable addition to your classroom and curriculum.

Standards

Each lesson in *Media Literacy, Grade 5*, meets one or more of the following standards, which are used with permission from McREL (Copyright 2007, McREL, Mid-continent Research for Education and Learning. Telephone: 303/337-0990.)

Standard	Page Number
Understands connections among the various art forms and other disciplines	24–26, 71–76, 116–133
Demonstrates competence in writing scripts	54, 63, 76
Designs and produces informal and formal productions	54, 63, 76
Understands how informal and formal theater, film, television, and electronic media productions create and communicate meaning	54–83, 91–92, 94–96, 107–114, 128–133
Understands and applies media, techniques, and processes related to the visual arts	24–41, 55–70, 75–133
Knows a range of subject matter, symbols, and potential ideas in the visual arts	24–41, 55–70, 75–127
Understands the visual arts in relation to history and cultures	24–41, 58–59, 62, 75–83, 84–85, 107–109, 116–133
Understands the characteristics and merits of one's own artwork and the artwork of others	26, 33, 41, 63, 76, 83, 90, 106, 115, 120, 127
Understands that group and cultural influences contribute to human development, identity, and behavior	9-53, 55, 57–62, 64–67, 71–76, 80–83, 91–115, 116–127, 128–133
Understands and interprets written and spoken language on diverse topics from diverse media	9-76, 78, 84–90, 98–115
Presents information, concepts, and ideas to an audience of listeners or readers on a variety of topics	54, 63, 76, 83, 106, 115, 132–133
Understands traditional ideas and perspectives, institutions, professions, literary and artistic expressions, and other components of the target culture	24–26, 42–76, 91–133
Understands the United States territorial expansion between 1801 and 1861, and how it affected relations with external powers and Native Americans	117

Standards *(cont.)*

Standard	Page Number
Understands economic, social, and cultural developments in the contemporary United States	27–54, 58–62, 77–97, 117, 121, 123, 128–133
Uses the general skills and strategies of the writing process	23, 33, 41, 54, 62, 70, 75–76, 82–83, 88–90, 93, 105–106, 112, 113, 122, 124, 131–132
Uses reading skills and strategies to understand and interpret a variety of literary texts	9–133
Uses listening and speaking strategies for different purposes	54, 63, 76, 83, 132
Uses viewing skills and strategies to understand and interpret visual media	24–41, 55–70, 74–76, 84–90, 93–95, 97–127, 128–133
Understands the characteristics and components of the media	all
Understands and applies the basic principles of presenting an argument	83, 96
Contributes to the overall effort of a group	54, 63, 76, 83, 96, 106, 127, 132–133
Understands the relationships among science, technology, society, and the individual	42–83, 91–97, 128–133
Knows characteristics/uses of computer software programs.	113, 128–133
Knows environmental and external factors that affect individual and community health	20–41, 42–54, 64–67, 72, 74–75, 80–81, 83, 91–97, 99–100, 103–104, 107–110, 128–133
Understands the historical perspective	24–29, 34–35, 44–45, 49–51, 58–59, 62, 72, 74, 77, 84–85, 108–109, 116–127
Knows environmental and external factors that affect individual and community health	20–41, 42–54, 64–67, 72, 74–75, 80–81, 83, 91–97, 99–100, 103–104, 107–110, 128–133
Understands the historical perspective	24–29, 34–35, 44–45, 49–51, 58–59, 62, 72, 74, 77, 84–85, 108–109, 116–127
Knows environmental and external factors that affect individual and community health	20–41, 42–54, 64–67, 72, 74–75, 80–81, 83, 91–97, 99–100, 103–104, 107–110, 128–133
Understands the historical perspective	24–29, 34–35, 44–45, 49–51, 58–59, 62, 72, 74, 77, 84–85, 108–109, 116–127

What Is Media Literacy?

You see and hear media every day. The radio you wake up to is media. Your cereal box is media. The TV is media. So are a movie, a magazine, and a book!

> **Media =** the ways that people connect with each other.

A literate person knows a lot about a subject. You show literacy when you write or give a report.

> **Literacy =** knowing about a subject

A media literate person knows a lot about forms of media. Here is a list of the most common ones.

- billboards
- books
- e-mail
- magazines
- mail
- movies
- newspapers
- packages
- paintings
- photos
- print ads
- radio
- sculptures
- speeches
- television
- videogames
- websites

> **Media Literacy =** knowing a lot about the ways in which people connect with each other.

This book will teach you to be media literate as you move through the world. Enjoy!

Forms of Media

All kinds of media affect what we buy from day to day. Here are some examples.

- A fifth-grader opens a copy of his favorite magazine about horses. He sees an ad for a new bridle. The horse in the ad has won a blue ribbon in a show. The boy asks his parents if they will buy his horse a new bridle.

- An 11-year old girl sees a movie with her friends. There is a good song that plays while the main actor wins a surfing contest. The movie ends. The girl and her friend buy the music from the movie.

There are other times when media affects our minds. Here are some examples.

- An art student opens a book. He sees a picture by a famous artist. The picture is of a young man who is very thin and fit. The art student decides that being thin and fit is good. He begins to run every day.

- A fifth-grade girl reads her local newspaper. She sees a story about how a child ate carrots and got sick. The girl eats a piece of her father's carrot cake and feels ill. She decides never to eat carrots again.

How Much Media

How much media do you watch or see every day? How much media do you hear?

Directions: Study the example below, and then fill out your own chart.

Joey Lopez's Media Chart

Type of Media	Hours Seen or Heard
Television	2 hours a day
Radio	1.5 hours a day
Books	4 hours a day

Your Media Chart

Type of Media	Hours Seen or Heard
Television	
Radio	
Internet	
Videogames	
Books	
Magazines	
Newspapers	
Billboards	
Other	

Why Does Media Matter?

Media tells us to buy one brand of shoes. It tells us to eat one type of ice cream. It even lets us know that if we dance one way, we will be happy.

The people who make media know that it has power. They see that if they put a fluffy kitten in an ad for milk, we will want to buy a carton. They know that if a popular singer wears one kind of shirt, we will want to wear that shirt, too.

Directions: Look at your chart from page 10. What is your favorite form of media? Write it in this space:

_____

Your favorite form of media makes you feel good. A girl who loves music feels happy when she listens to her radio. A boy who likes comic books is glad when a new comic book hits the stands.

How does your favorite form of media make you feel? Describe your feelings in two or three sentences below. My favorite form of media makes me feel_____

_____

_____

_____

_____

Get to Know Media

Do you want to get to know a new student? Chances are you would ask that person all about him or herself to do that. Would you like to learn how to throw a ball? Try to break the throw down into small steps and then learn each of them.

You can get to know a form of media when you ask questions. You can understand it when you break it down into small pieces. People who are media literate ask themselves things when they see or hear a form of media. Here is a list of the questions they may ask.

- Who paid for this media?
- Who will like this media? Why?
- What is the clear message in this media?
- What is the hidden message in this media?
- Is this healthy or unhealthy media?

Sara is a fifth-grade student. She opens up a magazine and sees an ad for a pair of boots. This is what she writes:

1. A brand called Bootiful Boots paid for this ad.

2. Girls will like this ad. There is a pretty girl in the ad. There are flowers and birds. The boots are pink.

3. The clear message in this ad is to "buy these boots."

4. The hidden message in this ad is "you will be pretty if you buy these boots."

5. This is healthy media.

Media Tricks

Media tricks are the way in which the people who make media get you to want what they sell.

Directions: Study the media tricks in this chart and read the examples to show how these tricks work.

Trick	Example
Bandwagon—this tricks says everyone else is buying an idea or a thing.	Everyone wears these sneakers. You should, too!
Beautiful People—good-looking models make us think we can look like them.	I'll look like him if I wear this shirt.
Bribes—we will get something we want if we buy a thing or idea.	Buy this toy and you will never be bored again.
Facts—facts and charts make us think that we should buy something.	Four out of five doctors recommend this vitamin for children.
Fear—something bad will happen if we don't buy what the media sells.	If you do not buy this toothpaste, your teeth will turn yellow.
Flattery—say something nice about people and you can get them to buy an idea or thing.	You are wise and so you know you need this brand of orange juice.
Humor—make people laugh, and you can sell anything!	This television ad for soda is funny. I want to buy that soda right now.
Hyperbole—something seems bigger or more exciting than it really is.	Blue's Blue Jeans will last a lifetime.
Name-calling—someone makes fun of someone else to sell a thing or idea.	Do not vote for Mary Myers because she is a mean lady and she will not listen to your needs.
Plain Folks—people in ads who look just like us make us want to be like them.	That boy with the brand-name tennis racket looks like me. I should buy that racket.
Repeating—when we hear a brand name or idea over and over, it sticks in our head.	Buy Benny's Berries because Benny's Berries are picked by Benny!
Symbol—a word, place, picture, or song that means something else, too.	This gold star is a symbol of good work.
Testimonials—famous people sell things and ideas.	This well-known baseball player uses this type of toothpaste. I should, too!
Warm and Fuzzy—cute, sweet images sell stuff.	That little puppy likes this brand of dog food. My dog will, too.

Slogans and Jingles

A slogan is a short phrase. It helps to sell a product or idea. Here are two well-known slogans to sell ideas.

- Give a hoot—don't pollute!
- Only you can prevent forest fires.

And here are two slogans to sell products.

- Stone's Sneakers will rock your world!
- Chill-Bear Ice Cream keeps you cool.

Below, write your favorite slogan for a product or idea:

_____

_____

A **jingle** is a little song. Jingles also help to sell a product or idea. Here is an example. Sing it to the tune of Row, Row, Row Your Boat.

Buy, buy, buy our cake.

It is really sweet.

Lemon, berry, or vanilla…

It is such a treat!

Advertisers hope that a jingle will stay in your mind and tempt you to buy their product.

Below, write a jingle from an ad on the television, radio, or in a film.

_____

_____

_____

_____

_____

_____

_____

_____

_____

Messages in Media

Each form of media has a message. There are two kinds of messages: clear and hidden.

You see or hear a clear media message right away. A magazine ad that shows a smiling boy on a brand-name surfboard gives you a clear message to buy the same surfboard.

A hidden message is harder to find. You have to look and listen to media carefully. The hidden message in the surfboard ad might say that if you buy this brand of board, you will be happy like the boy in the picture.

Can you find clear and hidden messages in media?

Directions: Study the descriptions below. Write one clear message and one hidden message for each form.

1. The star of a movie wears Sassy Girl blue jeans. All the boys like her. The girls want to be like her. The movie star gets good grades. She is also pretty. The camera shows the brand name of her jeans three times in the movie.

Clear Message	Hidden Message

2. A videogame has pictures of Quick-Fix hamburgers. The kids in the videogame have to eat as many hamburgers as they can before the doctor catches them. The more burgers your character eats, the more points you earn.

Clear Message	Hidden Message

Propaganda

People can use false claims to help sell a product or idea. This is called **propaganda**.

An ad with the slogan, "This cell phone will make you popular," is propaganda.

A television show with the slogan, "Get into the right college or you will fail," is propaganda.

Directions: Study the poster on the right from World War II. Then choose the letter that best completes each sentence.

Image courtesy of the Library of Congress, Prints and Photographs Division (LC-USZC4-5604)

1. This poster will appeal mostly to

   a. boys.   b. women.   c. husbands.   d. pilots.

2. The media trick in this poster is

   a. plain folks.   b. bribery.   c. flattery.   d. repeating.

3. The propaganda in this poster says

   a. women should   b. women cannot   c. if women work,   d. women make
      stay home.   be soldiers.   we will win the war.   good nurses.

Find Propaganda

Remember that propaganda makes a false claim to sell an idea or a product.

Directions: Study the ads in a magazine or newspaper. Find one ad that uses propaganda. Draw a picture of the ad in the space below. Then, answer the questions.

1. What product or idea does this ad sell?

   _____

   _____

   _____

2. What media trick does this ad use?

   _____

   _____

   _____

3. How does this ad use propaganda?

   _____

   _____

   _____

   _____

   _____

Now, make your own ad. Use propaganda. Choose an idea or product that you want to sell. Draw an ad on a piece of paper. Include a slogan and an image that show propaganda.

Stereotypes

A stereotype describes one kind of person with broad details. It is untrue. Stereotypes may play on the way someone looks. Here are a few examples.

She's a dumb blond.

Boys don't cry.

He has a wicked stepmother.

Stereotypes can hurt people. A blond girl may start to think that she is dumb. A boy may think he is not allowed to cry. And a stepmother may worry that she is not kind.

Can you find stereotypes in the media around you?

Directions: Study the examples of media below. Write down who is stereotyped in each example. Then explain who this media might hurt.

1. The star of a television show about detectives is tall and handsome. His sidekick is short and fat. The star makes fun of him. The sidekick says dumb things and makes a lot of mistakes.

Who is Stereotyped?	Who Might Be Hurt?

2. The rich girl in a novel for children is happy. She has many friends. The poor girl in the book is not happy. She is lonely. The other girls make fun of her cheap clothes and shoes.

Who is Stereotyped?	Who Might Be Hurt?

Stereotype or Original?

A stereotyped description gives a general, false idea of someone. An original description gives a specific, true idea of someone.

Directions: Fill in the chart below. On the left, create a stereotype for the character. On the right, create an original description. The first one has been done for you.

Character	Form of Media	Stereotype	Original
Police Officer	Magazine ad	This ad shows a white man. He is handsome and tall and thin. He has big muscles. He frowns as he gives a driver a ticket.	This ad shows a Latina woman. She is short. She smiles as she helps a little boy catch his puppy who slipped out of its leash.
Teacher	Television commercial		
Kung-Fu master	Videogame		

Healthy Media

Healthy media makes people feel good. It sends a positive message. It also helps people. A radio show that lets young writers read their poems on the air is an example of healthy media.

Unhealthy media can make people feel bad or sad. It sends a negative message. It can hurt people. Graffiti that uses bad words and calls someone names is an example of unhealthy media.

DEPARTMENT OF THE INTERIOR, NATIONAL PARK SERVICE

THE NATIONAL PARKS PRESERVE WILD LIFE

Directions: Study this poster from the 1930s. Answer true or false to the sentences below.

Image courtesy of the Library of Congress, Prints and Photographs Division (LC-USZC2-5639)

1. The clear message of this poster is that we should shoot mountain goats.

   True   False

2. The hidden message of this poster is that nature is beautiful.

   True   False

3. The media trick in this poster is hyperbole.

   True   False

4. This poster is a healthy form of media because it does not hurt anyone.

   True   False

Healthy Media *(cont.)*

Can you tell the difference between healthy and unhealthy media?

Directions: Study the ad below. Then, circle the word that best completes each sentence.

1. This ad is trying to sell

   bicycles   cell phones

2. "Live Dangerously" is a

   jingle   slogan

3. The media trick in this ad is

   warm and fuzzy fear

4. This ad is

   healthy   unhealthy

Now, it's your turn. In the left-hand column, draw a healthy poster for a new movie. In the right, draw an unhealthy poster for the same movie.

Healthy Media	Unhealthy Media

First Media

Petroglyphs are paintings or carvings on rocks. They use symbols. Symbols are pictures that stand for a thing or idea. Prehistoric people told stories with symbols.

They made these pictures long before pencils, pens, and paper. They used petroglyphs to talk about animals and weather. They also used them to talk about each other.

This petroglyph was made near Camp Verde, in Arizona.

Image courtesy of the Library of Congress, Prints and Photographs Division (LC-USZ62-113247)

Directions: Study the petroglyph. Can you guess what story the creator of this media wanted to tell? Write one possible story in the space below.

More on Petroglyphs

Now it is your turn to discover a petroglyph!

Directions: Find one petroglyph in a book, encyclopedia, or on the Internet. Draw the petroglyph in the space below, and then fill out the chart.

1. Found at:

_____

_____

2. Created by:

_____

_____

_____

3. Story behind the petroglyph:

_____

_____

_____

_____

_____

_____

Make a Petroglyph

The Native Americans made symbols to stand for ideas and things. Now it's your turn to create a petroglyph of your own. Send a message to your friends! You will need a small rock with one flat side and a small, sturdy stick or metal carving tool (alternately, you may use paint and brushes).

Directions:

1. Fill out the symbol-chart below. In the top row, write the words and/or ideas you will use on your petroglyph. On the bottom row, draw a symbol for each word. See the example below.

Word	Happy						
Symbol	☺						

2. Use the stick or metal carving tool to carve symbols into your rock. Or, you may paint your symbols on your rock.

3. Set out your petroglyph for others to see. See if they can understand your symbols.

4. On the lines below, write the message on your petroglyph.

_____

_____

_____

_____

_____

_____

_____

_____

_____

_____

_____

_____

_____

_____

Print Ads

A print ad is an ad that is on paper. It can be in newspaper or a magazine. It can be on a flier, too.

Print ads are one form of media. They use words and pictures to send a message.

Directions: Study this print ad from 1860. Circle the letter that best answers each question.

Image courtesy of the Library of Congress, Prints and Photographs Division (LC-USZ62-4624)

1. This is an ad for
   a. hot chocolate.   b. dresses.   c. a hair product.   d. families.

2. The media trick in this ad is
   a. fear.   b. bribery.   c. plain folks.   d. beautiful people.

3. This ad would appeal to people who
   a. want nice hair.   b. are bald.   c. don't have extra money to spend.   d. do not have time for hair-care.

Early Print Ads

Print ads have helped people to advertise their products and ideas for hundreds of years.

Directions: Study this print ad from 1869. It advertises conditioning powder to make your horses and cattle strong and beautiful. Answer true or false to the statements below.

Image courtesy of the Library of Congress, Prints and Photographs Division (LC-USZ62-463)

1. This print ad would appeal most to little kids.

   True   False

2. The brand name of this condition powder is "Harvell's."

   True   False

3. The media trick in this ad is beautiful people.

   True   False

4. The message in this ad is "buy this conditioning powder and your horse will get sick."

   True   False

5. The building to the left of the horse symbolizes a racetrack.

   True   False

Are you ready to analyze a print ad all on your own?

Directions: Study the ad below, and then fill in the blanks for each sentence at the bottom of the page.

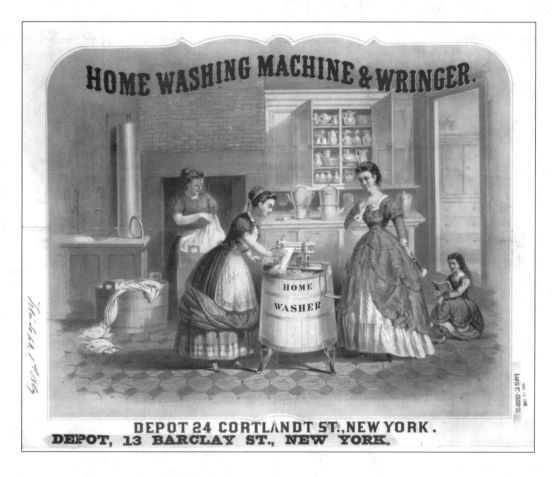

Image courtesy of the Library of Congress, Prints and Photographs Division (LC-USZ62-2589)

1. This is an ad for

_____

2. This print ad will appeal mostly to

_____

3. The clear message of this ad is

_____

_____

4. The stereotype in this ad suggests that

_____

_____

Print Ads of Today

Print ads have changed over the years. The next two pages ask you to study a print ad of today.

Directions: Find a print ad in a magazine or newspaper. Cut it out and paste it into the space below. Or, you may choose to draw the ad in the space below.

Print Ads of Today (cont.)

Directions: Study the print ad you pasted or drew on page 28. Answer the questions below.

1. Who paid for this ad?

   _____

2. What type of person would like this ad?

   _____

3. Is there a slogan? If so, write it here.

   _____

   _____

4. What media trick does this ad use?

   _____

   _____

5. What is the clear message in this ad?

   _____

   _____

   _____

6. What is the hidden message in this ad?

   _____

   _____

   _____

   _____

7. Is this ad an example of healthy or unhealthy media?

   _____

   _____

Same and Different

How have the pictures in print ads changed over time? How have the words in print ads changed? How have ads stayed the same over hundreds of years?

Directions: Find an early print ad in a book, encyclopedia, or on the Internet. Possible search engine words include *early print advertisements*, *historical advertisements*, and *pictorial Americana*.

Draw the ad you find on a sheet of paper.

Find a print ad from this year in a magazine or newspaper. Draw this ad on another sheet of paper.

Study the two ads and then answer the questions below.

1. How are the words in these two ads the same?

   _____

   _____

2. How are the words in these two ads different?

   _____

   _____

3. How are the pictures in these two ads the same?

   _____

   _____

4. How are the pictures in these two ads different?

   _____

   _____

   _____

   _____

5. How are the messages in these two ads the same?

   _____

   _____

   _____

   _____

6. How are the messages in these two ads different?

   _____

   _____

   _____

   _____

Make Your Own Print Ad

Show what you have learned about print ads. Make your own! You will need a blank sheet of paper, pens or pencils, and a ruler.

Directions: Design your own print ad on a sheet of paper. Make sure it has the following things.

- slogan
- media trick
- message
- brand name

Now, answer the questions below about your ad.

1. What product or idea do you advertise?

_____

2. What is your slogan?

_____

3. What group will like your ad the most?

_____

_____

4. What media trick do you use in your ad?

_____

_____

5. What are the messages in your ad?

_____

_____

_____

_____

6. Is your ad an example of healthy or unhealthy media?

_____

_____

_____

_____

_____

Billboards

Billboards are huge print ads. A "bill" was once another name for an ad. You can find billboards on the walls of buildings. You can also find them along roads and highways. They have been around since the mid-1800s.

The photograph below was taken in 1922. It shows how billboards were a popular form of advertising.

Image Courtesy of
RC Maxwell Collection – Database #M0400
Emergence of Advertising On-Line Project
John W. Hartman Center for Sales, Advertising & Marketing History
Duke University Rare Book, Manuscript, and Special Collections Library
http://library.duke.edu/digitalcollections/eaa/

How many products do you see advertised in this photo? Write the number here. _____

Early Billboards

A famous photographer named Dorothea Lange took a photo of this billboard in 1937.

Image courtesy the Library of Congress, Prints and Photographs Division (LC-DIG-fsa-8b31722)

Directions: Study the billboard. Draw a line from each term to the correct description.

1. clear message   a. "There's no way like the American Way."

2. what is being sold   b. world's shortest working hours

3. hidden message   c. if you live in America, you will go on a picnic.

4. slogan   d. America is special

5. propaganda   e. the American Way.

Idea Billboards

Some billboards advertise ideas instead of products.

Directions: Study this billboard from 1922. What is The Lions Club? Type the words "Lions Service Club" into your favorite search engine to find out. Write a one-sentence description of the club in the space below.

RC Maxwell Collection - Database #M0331
Emergence of Advertising On-Line Project
John W. Hartman Center for Sales, Advertising & Marketing History
Duke University Rare Book, Manuscript, and Special Collections Library
http://library.duke.edu/digitalcollections/eaa/

1. Trenton Manufacturers paid for this billboard.

   True   **False**

2. This billboard says that people should not become American Citizens.

   True   **False**

3. On this billboard, the "Republic" means the United States.

   True   **False**

4. The media trick on this billboard is fear.

   True   **False**

Political Billboards

The political billboard below, created in 1948, is a campaign billboard.

Directions: Study this billboard from 1948. Fill in the blank spaces below to complete each sentence.

Image courtesy of The National Archives (187021)

1. This billboard was likely paid for by the _____ Party.

2. The clear message of this billboard is that you should _____

   _____

3. The slogan of this billboard is _____

   _____

4. This billboard will appeal to _____

5. One hidden message on this billboard might be _____

   _____

Billboards of Today

What billboards do you see every day in your city or town?

Directions: Choose a billboard from your city. Draw it in the box below. Answer the questions below.

1. Who paid for this billboard?

_____

2. What idea or product is advertised?

_____

3. Who would like this billboard?

_____

_____

4. What media trick is used?

_____

_____

5. What is the clear message on this billboard?

_____

_____

6. What is the hidden message on this billboard?

_____

_____

Compare and Contrast

Think about billboards from the past and from today. Can you see how this form of media has changed over the years?

Directions: Find a photograph of a billboard made before 1970. Use encyclopedias, books, and the Internet. Try search engine words such as *history of billboards*, *billboard ads*, and *early billboards*.

Draw the billboard in the space below.

Compare and Contrast *(cont.)*

Directions: Look again at your drawing of a billboard from your city. Compare it to your drawing of a billboard from the past. Write a short report on how billboards have changed over the past decades.

In your report, write about the following:

- words
- pictures
- slogans

- messages
- media tricks
- healthy or unhealthy media

Make Your Own Billboard

Show what you have learned about billboards! Make your own billboard. You will need two-to-three pieces of scrap paper, butcher paper (two sheets six feet long each), transparent tape (one piece six feet long), pencils with erasers, and markers or paint and brushes.

Directions: Get into groups of three or four. Discuss what ad will be on your billboard. Will it be an ad for an idea or a product? On scrap paper, draw what the billboard will look like.

Lay the pieces of butcher paper out on the carpet. Put one above the other. Tape them together at their longest end. You should have a large rectangle.

Draw your billboard on the butcher paper. Make sure to add pictures and text.

Use markers or paint and brushes to add color to your billboard. Let it dry. Then show it off in a hallway or a classroom.

Once complete, answer these questions about your billboard.

1. What product or idea does your billboard sell?

   _____

   _____

2. What media trick do you use?

   _____

   _____

3. What is the clear message of your billboard?

   _____

   _____

4. What is the hidden message of your billboard, if any?

   _____

   _____

5. Is your billboard an example of healthy or unhealthy media? Why?

   _____

   _____

   _____

   _____

Radio

Radio gives us music. It gives us news. It even gives us plays and stories. It has been around for over 100 years.

1887 ⟶ Scientist Heinrich Hertz finds radio waves!

1918 ⟶ Radio stations give news about politics!

1919 ⟶ Companies make hundreds of "radio music boxes."

1920 ⟶ Now there are radio broadcasts each night from 8:30–9:30 P.M.!

1922 ⟶ There are 500 radio stations!

1933 ⟶ The Lone Ranger radio show begins on radio.

1944 ⟶ The Roy Rogers radio show begins on radio.

1960s ⟶ Transistor radios become popular.

2000 ⟶ People can download music off the Internet.

Image courtesy of The National Archives (536540)

1942—Photograph of Henry Tambora repairing a radio in his shop, Washington State, U.S.A.

Radio Ads

Print ads appeal to our eyes. Radio ads appeal to our ears. A print ad can show a fuzzy kitten or a shiny car. A radio ad has to use sounds instead of pictures.

On the radio, you can hear the kitten mew. You can hear the tires on the car race around a track. In what other ways might the radio use sound?

Directions: Look at the chart below. Think of how you might use sound to show media tricks. Fill out the chart. The first one has been done for you.

1. Warm and fuzzy	You could use a baby's voice and a lullaby, or a puppy's little bark. Voices could say, "Oh, how cute!"
2. Fear	
3. Beautiful people	
4. Symbols	
5. Humor	
6. Repetition	
7. Facts	

Radio Ads from the Past

You can hear radio ads from the past on the Internet.

Directions: Ask your teacher or a parent to help you locate an Internet search engine. Use the search terms *Old Radio Commercials* or *Historic Radio Commercials*.

Listen to two radio ads from the past, and then answer the questions below.

Question	Commercial One	Commercial Two
A. What product is this radio ad trying to sell, and what is the brand name?		
B. Who would like this radio ad?		
C. What media trick does this radio ad use?		
D. What sounds does this radio ad use?		
E. What is the clear message of this radio ad?		
F. What is the hidden message of this radio ad?		
G. Is this radio commercial healthy or unhealthy?		

Radio Ads of Today

How have radio ads changed? How have they stayed the same? Do they use more jokes? More music? Less words? Less sounds?

Directions: Listen to two ads on your radio at school or at home. Fill in the charts below and on the next page.

Question	Ad One	Ad Two
A. What product is this radio ad trying to sell, and what is the brand name?		
B. Who would like this radio ad?		
C. What media trick does this radio ad use?		
D. What sounds does this radio ad use?		
E. What is the clear message of this radio ad?		
F. What is the hidden message of this radio ad?		
G. Is this radio commercial healthy or unhealthy?		

Record a Radio Ad

Now it's your turn to write and make a radio ad! You will need lined paper, a pen or pencil, and a tape recorder or computer with voice recording ability.

Directions: Get into a group of four students. Decide on a product or idea that you would like to sell. Talk about how long to make your radio ad. Radio ads are short. They range from 15- and 30- to 60-second spots.

Write a script for your ad and decide who will play what part. For ideas, see the extract of a script below.

Buyer: I would like to buy a basketball.

Seller: I have just the thing for you.

(Sound of a ping-pong ball hitting the floor)

Buyer: But this is a ping-pong ball!

Seller: It is on sale!

Decide if you will you need sound effects, and find items that will make interesting sounds. Practice your ad a few times until you are happy then record it. You may need to record several times to get it right.

Now write one paragraph about your ad on a separate sheet of paper. You may do this alone or as a group. Make sure you include the following items:

- your product
- who will like your ad
- media tricks
- sounds you used

- clear messages
- hidden messages
- healthy or unhealthy media

Finally, play your radio commercial for your class!

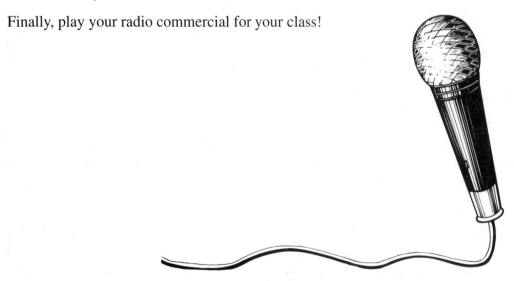

Radio Shows from the Past

A radio show can last half an hour or an hour. Old radio shows had music. They had plays. They also had comedy.

Here are names of some of the most famous radio shows:

- "Hopalong Cassidy"
- "Amos and Andy"
- "Cloak and Dagger"
- "The Green Hornet"

You can find a copy of an old radio show at some libraries. You can also hear them on the Internet.

Directions: Go to your local library and check out a copy of two different radio shows on CD or on audiotape. Or find two old radio shows on the Internet. Type the words *old time radio show* or *radio programs* into your favorite Internet search engine.

Describe the first show by filling in the blanks in the script below.

Radio Show One

Boy: What are you listening to? _____

Girl: I am listening to a radio show called _____

Boy: What kinds of sounds does it use? _____

Girl: Oh, I can hear sounds like _____ and _____

Boy: Just who would like this radio show, anyway? _____

Girl: Why, people who are _____

Boy: Is there a clear message in this radio show? _____

Girl: Yes. It is _____

_____

Boy: What media trick is used on this show? _____

Girl: The show uses the trick _____

_____

Directions: Listen to the second radio show. Describe it by filling in the blanks in the script below.

Radio Show Two

Woman: Say, what's that you're listening to?

Man: It's a show called _____

Woman: Is it a healthy form of media?

Man: Well, I feel that this show is _____

Woman: Who likes to listen to this show?

Man: Oh, people who are _____ and _____

Woman: I hear something strange. What sounds does this show use?

Man: I hear _____, _____, and _____ on this show.

Woman: So what media trick is used in this show?

Man: I think the media trick is _____

Woman: I wonder if there is a hidden message on this show.

Man: Oh, yes. It is _____

_____

Woman: What is the clear message of this radio show?

Man: If you listen, you'll hear that the show tells us to _____

_____

War of the Worlds

The War of the Worlds is the name of a science fiction book. In 1938, a man named Orson Welles read part of this book on the radio. He scared people!

It was the day before Halloween. Orson read a part of the book that sounded like radio news. This pretend news said that Martians had invaded the Earth.

People thought this was true. They did not realize it was only a story. They hid in their houses. They tried to drive away. They thought the Martians would kill them with poison gas.

How did a radio show start such a panic?

Directions: Listen to the first five minutes of Orson Welles' broadcast of *The War of the Worlds*. You can find it at some libraries. You can also find it on the Internet.

Type these words into your favorite search engine: *War of the Worlds radio*, or *Orson Welles War of the Worlds*. This will give you a link so you can hear the show.

Listen to the first five minutes of the show. Then answer the questions below in complete sentences.

1. What is this story about?	
2. What parts of this radio show made people think that Martians had come down to Earth?	
3. Do you think that the same panic could happen today from a radio show? Explain your answer.	

Radio Shows for Children

Children have listened to radio shows for a long time. Old radio shows had superheroes and cowboys. These shows ended with a cliffhanger. A cliffhanger left the hero in danger at the end of the show. This made children want to listen to the show the next day.

The radio shows of today are a little different. You can find some of them on the computer. They are called podcasts. You can put a podcast on your own headphones and listen to it whenever you want to!

Directions: Listen to two radio shows for children. You may use your radio. You may also use the Internet. Type these words into your favorite search engine: *radio shows for kids*, *children's podcast*, or *children's radio shows*. When you have finished listening, fill in the chart below.

Question	Radio Program One	Radio Program Two
1. Who will like this show—boys or girls or both?		
2. How does this radio show use sound?		
3. What media trick is used in this radio show?		
4. What is the clear message of this radio show?		
5. What is the hidden message of this radio show?		
6. Is this radio show a healthy or unhealthy form of media?		

Record Your Radio Show

Now it's your turn to write and record a five- to ten-minute radio show. You will need several sheets of lined paper, a pen or pencil, a tape recorder or computer that can record, and things to use for sound effects.

Directions: Get into a group of four students. Decide what you will put on your radio show. Will you teach children how to do something on your show? Maybe they will learn to sing or to speak Spanish? Will you talk with guests? Maybe you will talk with the principal or with a parent who owns a bakery?

Write a script for your radio show and decide who will play what parts. Think about whether you will need sound effects. Find objects that will make these sounds. Practice your radio show a few times until you are happy with it and then record it. You may need to record several takes. Finally, answer the questions below. Don't forget to play your radio commercial for your class!

1. What is the name of your radio show?

   _____

2. How does your radio show use sound?

   _____

   _____

3. What media trick does your radio show use?

   _____

   _____

4. Who will like your radio show the most?

   _____

   _____

5. What clear messages are on your show?

   _____

   _____

   _____

6. Are there any hidden messages? If so, what are they?

   _____

   _____

   _____

Television

Radio let people hear media. But they wanted to see media, too. Enter the television! Television has a long history. Here are some of the most interesting milestones.

1862	→	The first image is sent over wires.
1927	→	New York City broadcasts a television image that is seen in Washington, D.C.
1929	→	The first television studio opens.
1936	→	The world has about 200 hundred television sets in use.
1939	→	The New York World's Fair shows television. They rely on a radio for sound.
1948	→	One million homes in the United States have television sets.
1956	→	The first remote control is invented. It is called the Zenith Space Commander.
1966	→	The first satellite shows television across the world.
1967	→	Most television programs are in color.
1969	→	Six hundred million people watch the first television broadcast from the moon.
1981	→	High-definition television gave viewers better picture quality.
1990s	→	1990s—Closed-captioning allows hearing-impaired viewers to better enjoy television.
Today	→	Today—There are at least 1.7 billion television sets around the world!

Your Television Log

How much do you watch television? Do you watch three hours a day? Half an hour a day? Do you like one show or one channel?

Directions: Write down your television habits for seven days. Fill out the television log below. Write down what you watched each day. Write down how long you watched television, too. Your log should look like this example.

Day of Week	What I Watched	How Long I Watched
Sunday	nature program cartoon	one hour ½ hour

Day of Week	What I Watched	How Long I Watched
Sunday		
Monday		
Tuesday		
Wednesday		
Thursday		
Friday		
Saturday		

No television in your house? Write one page to explain why. Write down what you think of television and if you would like to have a television… or not.

Television Ads

The first television ad showed in 1941. It was a 10-second commercial for wristwatches. The Bulova Watch Company paid seven dollars to put its ad on television. The ad sold a lot of watches. Then, everyone wanted to put an ad on television!

In 1952, television ads showed the childrens' toy called "Mr. Potato Head®." That year, the toy company made four million dollars in sales. Television ads are powerful media tools.

Some television ads use jingles. Some use slogans. Some use animals. Others use cute kids. Television ads try to sell us items. They may also try to sell us ideas. They have clear and hidden messages just like any other form of media.

Now people watch over 40,000 television ads each year. Do you have a favorite television ad? Write about it in the space below. Write five to seven sentences.

My Favorite Television Ad

_____

_____

_____

_____

_____

Television Ads from the Past

In the past, television ads were long. Just one television ad could run for a minute and a half. Now television ads are very short. They may only run for 30 seconds. Some may be as short as 15 seconds!

What did these old television ads look like? Were they silly? Were they helpful? Watch two and find out!

Directions: Find two television ads from the past on the Internet. Look for ads from the 1940s, 1950s, and the 1960s.

Type one or more of these phrases into your favorite search engine: *classic commercials*, *old commercials*, or *television commercials*.

Once you have watched both ads, write a short essay to describe them. In your essay, make sure to answer the questions below.

- What do the ads try to sell?
- Who will like these ads?
- What media tricks do these ads use?
- What are the clear messages of these ads?
- What are the hidden messages of these ads?
- Are these ads examples of healthy or unhealthy media?

Television Ads of Today

How have television ads changed over time? Some products are not allowed to be shown on television now. Ads for cigarettes have been banned from television since the 1970s. This is because cigarettes can cause cancer. Television stations can still show ads for alcohol, but they can not show people actually drinking.

We see more ads today than people saw in the 1960s. Back then, a hour of television looked like this.

Television show = 51 minutes long

Television ads = 9 minutes long

Now, an hour of television looks like this.

Television show = 42 minutes long

Television ads = 18 minutes long

You can see that there are more ads now than ever before. What else about television ads has changed?

Directions: Watch two television ads at school or at home, and complete the chart below. When you have finished, write a short essay on a separate piece of paper. Tell about which ads you saw. Do you like the ads from the past or do you prefer television ads from the present? Explain your answer.

What does this ad try to sell?		
Who will like this ad?		
What media trick does this ad use?		
What is the clear message of this ad?		
What is the hidden message of this ad?		
Is this ad healthy or unhealthy?		

Compare and Contrast

Now you have seen four television ads. You have seen two from the past and two from the present. Show how they have changed over time.

Directions: Make a Venn diagram. Show how television ads from the past and present are the same. Show how they are different. Think about the following things.

- products
- music
- humor
- voices
- people
- places

Study the example below, and then complete your own Venn diagram on page 56.

Television Ads from the Past

Television Ads of the Present

long dresses and long pants
no music
lots of talking

an announcer
a pet dog
selling shampoo

bathing suits
hip-hop music
no talking

Compare and Contrast *(cont.)*

Directions: Make a Venn diagram. Show how television ads from the past and present are the same. Show how they are different. Think about the following things.

- products
- music
- humor
- voices
- people
- places

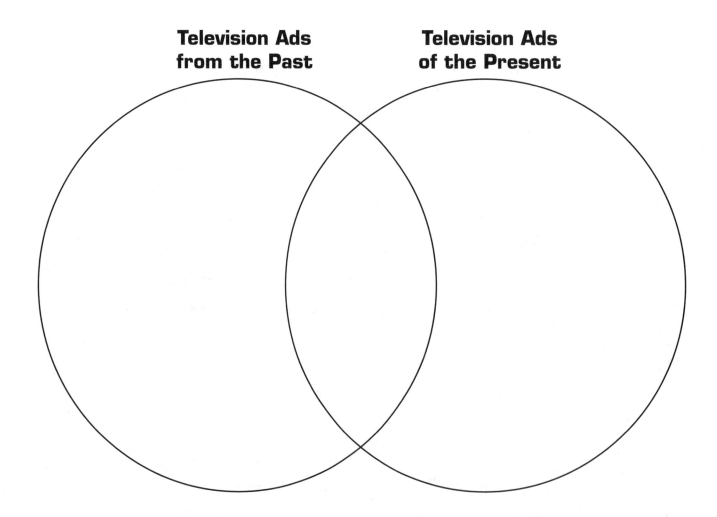

Television Ads from the Past

Television Ads of the Present

Make a Television Ad

Now it is your turn to make a television ad! You will need 4–5 sheets of lined paper, a pen or pencil, a video recorder or computer with video recording capability, and costumes and props.

Directions: Get into a group of three-to-four students. Talk about what you will sell on your television ad. Will you tell a story? Sing a song? Do a dance? How will you get people to buy what you are selling?

Write a script for your ad. Decide who will play what parts. Decide on a director and actors. Find costumes and props. See the example script below for ideas on how to write your ad.

Practice your ad until you are happy, then record it. You may need to record several takes to get it just right.

Sample Script

Dad: Son! You have lost your backpack again.

Mom: And where are your shoes?

Boy: I don't know! I thought I knew where they were.

Announcer: Feeling bad because you lose everything? Then buy our "Here I Am" sticker. Just stick it to an item. If you lose that item, clap your hands. The sticker will cry "Here I am!" Then you can find your item!

Now fill out the chart below for your television ad.

Audience?	
Product or Idea You Are Selling?	
How do you Use Sound?	
Obvious Messages?	
Hidden Messages?	
Healthy or Unhealthy?	

Television News

Do you or your parents wake up to the morning news on television? Do you come home from a busy day and turn on the news?

TV news has been on since 1948. Reporters talk about wars and sports. They talk about elections and animal stories, health problems, car chases, and break-ins.

Some people say that television news is too violent. It uses scary stories to get people to tune in. News writers sometimes say "If it bleeds, it leads." This means that news—both on television and in the paper—begins with a scary story.

Directions: Watch the first five minutes of three news programs on television. On the chart below, record what you find. The first one has been done for you.

Name of News Program	Topic of Lead Story	What is the Lead Story About?
KLXM Morning News	A school was broken into.	Teachers got to school to find that their rooms had been broken into. Someone stole books and desks. And the walls had been spray-painted.

Healthy or Unhealthy?

How do you feel when you watch television news? Do you feel sad or scared? Happy or mad? Which news stories are healthy forms of media? Which are unhealthy?

Directions: Watch one half-hour of news on television. Fill out the chart below. Write about at least three news stories. Follow the example:

Name of news program watched: _____

Topic	Description	Healthy or Unhealthy?
Dog saves the life of a family.	A dog barked until a sleeping family woke up and saw that their house was on fire. The dog dragged a little boy outside to safety. The rest of the family got out alive, too.	Healthy. This is a piece that makes people feel good because it has a happy ending.

Television Advertisers

Television advertisers pay money for ads to run during a television program. They choose their programs with care. This is why ads for medicine and kitchen items run with soap operas. Television advertisers hope that women who watch these soap operas will buy their items. They hope that children who watch cartoons will buy items, too. This is why there are ads for toys and sweet treats in between television shows for children.

Directions: Watch a half-hour television show at school or at home. Below, make notes on what each commercial is trying to sell. Then answer the questions at the bottom of the page.

Name of television program: _____

Items advertised during the program:

_____

_____

_____

_____

_____

_____

_____

_____

1. Who will like this television program? _____

_____

2. What kind of item is advertised most often in the commercials during this program?

_____

_____

3. Why do you think the advertisers wanted to show commercials for their item along with this television program?

_____

_____

4. Are most of the items in these commercials healthy or unhealthy?

_____

_____

_____

Messages—Clear and Hidden

You know how to find clear messages in print ads and radio programs. You also know how to find hidden messages in these forms of media. Can you find clear and hidden messages in a television show?

Directions: Watch a half-hour long television show. Take notes on any clear and hidden messages you find. Study the example below.

Name of television show: _____

Clear messages	Hidden messages
The kids in the show drink Gloopy's Root Beer. The mom on the show uses a SmartWhiz computer.	The main character is tall and thin and pretty. The hidden message is that these things are good and important. The mom always does the dishes. The hidden message is that washing dishes is a woman's work.

Now, fill out the chart at the bottom of the page for your television show. Try to find at least four clear messages, and four hidden messages, too!

Name of television show: _____

Clear messages	Hidden messages

The Big Turnoff

How many hours of television do kids watch each year? 20? 100? Wrong! Children in the United States watch about 1,023 hours of television every year.

Television can teach us things. We can learn about history and science. We can learn about animals and sports. But too much television can also make us unhealthy.

Some adults started TV-Turnoff Week in 1994. They wanted to show that too much time watching television is not good for us. In the U.S.A., TV-Turnoff Week is the last week in April. Thousands of people all over the country do not watch television during that week.

The next three pages will help you to start your own TV-Turnoff Week!

How important is television in your life, on a scale of 1 to 10? Circle the number below.

1	2	3	4	5	6	7	8	9	10
not important				I enjoy it.					very important

Do you want to know what kinds of people started TV-Turnoff Week?

Directions: Use your favorite Internet search engine. In it, type the words *TV-Turnoff, television turnoff*, or *turn off your TV in April*. Ask your teacher to check the site you have chosen to make sure it is appropriate. Then, study the home page of one group's website. Fill in the chart below to study this website even more.

1. Who would like this website?	
2. What media tricks are used on this website?	
3. What clear messages do you see on this website?	
4. What hidden messages do you find on this website?	
5. Is this website healthy or unhealthy?	
6. Is TV-Turnoff Week a good idea? Why or why not?	

No TV? No Worries!

You have turned off your television for a week. Now what are you going to do? There are many things to do and try for this week. Why not ride your bike, learn to sew, or watch a spider make a web? You could help your parents cook dinner or train your parrot to talk!

Directions: Alone, or in groups of four, think about 20 things to do instead of watching television. Write your ideas in the spaces below.

1. _____

2. _____

3. _____

4. _____

5. _____

6. _____

7. _____

8. _____

9. _____

10. _____

11. _____

12. _____

13. _____

14. _____

15. _____

16. _____

17. _____

18. _____

19. _____

20. _____

TV-Turnoff Week Journal

Try not to watch any television for a week. Keep a journal in the space below. Write down how you felt every day without TV. Write down what you did instead.

Example

Today I rode my bike to Grandma's house. I helped in her garden. I also walked my dog. I missed watching cartoons, but it was fun to ride my bike.

JOURNAL

Day One

....
....
....
....

Day Two

....
....
....
....
....

Day Three

....
....
....
....

Day Four

....
....
....
....
....

Day Five

....
....
....
....

Day Six

....
....
....
....
....

Day Seven

....
....
....
....

Music

"The Itsy Bitsy Spider." "Row, Row, Row Your Boat." "Yankee Doodle." "The Star-Spangled Banner." You know dozens of songs from home and school. You probably know even more from the radio.

Music makes us feel happy and full of life. It can also make us feel serious or sad. It can be fast or slow. It can use instruments or just voices. Music is an important part of our lives. It is a form of media that we hear every day.

How do you feel about music?

Directions: Complete the sentences below.

1. My favorite kind of music is _____

2. My favorite song is _____
   _____

3. My favorite singer is _____
   _____

4. I like to listen to music when I am _____
   _____

5. I do not like to listen to music when I am _____
   _____

6. When I am in a bad mood, music _____
   _____

7. When I am in a good mood, music _____
   _____

65

Problems in Music

Sometimes music makes problems. And sometimes the people who make music have to deal with problems. Here are a few examples from history.

The 1920s ⟶ Parents worried about their kids listening to jazz music. They thought it would make their children smoke and drink and hang out with the wrong sorts of people.

The 1950s ⟶ Officials did not like the way that Elvis Presley danced. They said that if he danced on stage at a concert, they would stop the concert.

The 1960s ⟶ In New York, some students were forbidden to do the dance called "The Twist."

The 1980s ⟶ People formed the Parents Resource Music Center. They urged producers to rate new albums as healthy or unhealthy for kids.

The 1990s ⟶ Officials said that some music is not healthy for young people. They made a sticker to put on albums, tapes, and CDs.

The 2000s ⟶ City and school officials banned some rappers from having concerts. They worried that the rap songs were unhealthy for children to hear.

One music problem is called "file sharing." File sharing means that you pay for and download a song off the Internet. Then you share it with your friends for free. Your friends can save it to their computer and share it with even more people. It is illegal. Some people have been fined thousands of dollars for file sharing. Courts of law say that they have stolen music.

What do you think about file sharing? Do you think it is a good thing, a bad thing, or both?

Directions: In the space below, write a short essay answering the questions.

1. How can file sharing music help you? How can it hurt you?

2. How can file sharing music help a musician? How can it hurt a musician?

3. Now, think about a problem to do with music and describe it.

What Is This Song About?

A lot of people hear songs but do not ask what they are about. They like the music. Sometimes they do not even listen to the words! But words are as important to songs as drums and trumpets and guitars.

Directions: Pick your favorite song. Write the words in the space to the left. On the right side of the page, answer the questions.

1. What is this song about? _____

_____

_____

_____

2. Who would like this song? _____

_____

_____

_____

3. What clear messages do you hear in this song?

_____

_____

_____

4. What hidden messages do you hear in this song?

_____

_____

_____

5. How might someone feel after hearing this song?

_____

_____

_____

6. Is this song a healthy or unhealthy form of media?

_____

_____

Music Videos

Music videos are two-to-three minute movies that go with a song. The first music videos were made in the 1980s. Only a few bands made them. Now many bands make music videos to go with their songs!

A music video is a form of media. You can study them for clear and hidden messages. You can watch a music video and decide whether it is a healthy or unhealthy form of media.

Directions: Find a music video on the Internet. Show your teacher what you find before watching or ask your teacher to find one for you to watch.

Watch the video and think about what the band are trying to do and show. Think about the hidden and clear messages.

As you watch, write your thoughts or notes on the lines below showing what you think of the videos. Make sure you include the name of the band and the name of the song.

_____

_____

_____

_____

_____

_____

_____

_____

Music Videos *(cont.)*

Directions: Read the screenplay below of a short music video and then answer the questions.

Fade in:

A boy is trying to do a jump on his skateboard at a park. He keeps falling. A band plays on the grass beside the cement ramp.

Close-up On The Band

Song
"You say you can't do it.

You'll give up and go away.

But I know better, baby.

I'll help you if you stay."

Pan out:

A girl walks up to the park with her skateboard. She looks at the boy. He tries the jump again. He falls. She walks over to him and holds out her hand to help him up.

Close-up:

The girl does a perfect jump on her skateboard. She smiles. The boy tries another jump. This time, he makes it.

Pan out:

Show band members clapping their hands.

Fade out

1. Who would like this music video? _____

   _____

2. What media trick does this music video use? _____

   _____

3. What is the clear message in this music video? _____

   _____

4. What is the hidden message in this music video? _____

   _____

5. How might someone feel after watching this music video? _____

   _____

6. Is this music video a healthy or unhealthy example of media? _____

   _____

More on Music Videos

Music videos use symbols. They also use hidden messages. They use fear and bandwagon and other media tricks. They are just like any other kind of media.

Directions: Pick your favorite music video. Watch it and take notes. Pretend you are a music writer for a magazine or a newspaper. Write a review of this music video.

Remember that a review is more than just telling the story of the music video. In your review, you must write about the following items.

- what this video is about
- who would like it
- what media tricks are used

- the clear and hidden messages
- how people will feel after they watch this video
- whether it is an example of healthy or unhealthy media

Make a Music Video

Now you know all that happens within a music video. It is time to make one of your own! You will need sheets of lined paper, a pen or pencil, a video recorder or computer with video recording capability, and costumes and props.

Directions: Get into a group of five-to-six students. Decide what song you will use. Will you make a video for someone else's song? Will you come up with your own song and make a music video for it?

Write up a script for your video and decide who will play what parts. Choose a director, actors, and band members/singers, if needed. Decide if you will need costumes and props and then practice the video until you are happy with it.

Record your music video. You may need to record several takes. You can switch back and forth between filming your band members/singers and filming your actors.

Once you have finished your music video, answer the questions below.

1. What is your music video about? _____

_____

2. Who will like it?

_____

3. What media tricks do you use in your video?

_____

_____

4. What clear messages are in your video?

_____

_____

5. What hidden messages are in your video?

_____

_____

6. How will people feel after they watch your video?

_____

_____

7. Is your music video an example of healthy or unhealthy media?

_____

_____

Finally, play your music video for your class!

Videogames

Videogames let you pretend that you are in outer space. They give you super-human powers. They raise your heartbeat. They can even make your palms sweat!

Videogames have been around since the 1970s. The first videogame was called *Computer Space*. People went to arcades to play games like *Space Invaders*, *Frog*, and *Centipede*.

In 1972, people could play videogames on their television at home. They used a large joystick. The games had simple lines, circles, and sounds. *Pong* was one of the first home videogames.

Today's videogames have many pictures and sounds. They make you feel like you are in a different world. A console is the actual box that houses a videogame. It looks much different now than it did in the 1970s!

Directions: Here are pictures of a videogame console from the 1970s and one from the present.

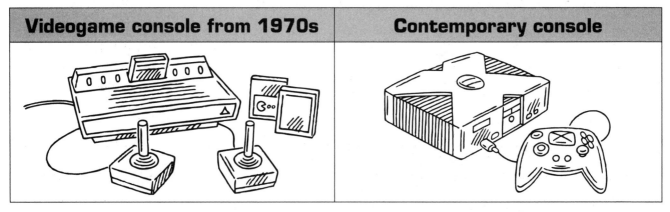

Videogame console from 1970s	Contemporary console

Compare the pictures and explain how these consoles have changed.

1. _____

_____

2. Why do you think people like to play videogames?

_____

_____

3. How often do you play videogames?

_____

_____

4. What is your favorite videogame? Why?

_____

_____

5. If you do not play videogames, explain why.

_____

_____

Videogame Ads

You can see videogame ads on television. You can see them when you go to a movie. You can see them in a magazine or a newspaper. How do these ads get you to buy one kind of video game?

The people who make ads for videogames are smart. They know just how to make their product exciting and fun.

Directions: Study the videogame ad below and then answer the questions.

1. What is the name of this videogame? _____

2. What company makes this videogame? _____

3. What is this company's slogan? _____

4. What media trick does this print ad use? _____

   _____

5. What is the clear message of this print ad? _____

   _____

6. What is the hidden message of this print ad? _____

   _____

7. Is this ad a healthy or unhealthy form of media? _____

   _____

Videogame Ads *(cont.)*

Now you know how to study an ad for a videogame. Put your skills into practice with your favorite ad.

Directions: Find an ad for a videogame. This may be a print ad from a newspaper or magazine. It may be a television ad or an Internet website.

Look at the ad you have chosen and answer the questions below.

1. What is this name of this videogame?	
2. What slogan does this advertisement use?	
3. What is the brand name of this videogame?	
4. Who will like this videogame?	
5. What media tricks does this ad use?	
7. What clear messages do you find in this ad?	
8. What hidden messages do you find in this ad?	
9. Is this ad an example of healthy or unhealthy media?	

Violent Videogames

Throw poison darts at a wizard! Kill the alien from Mars! Crash into as many cars as you can! In 1998, 80 percent of kids' favorite videogames were violent. They showed some sort of injury or death.

Most people who play videogames see fake blood and killings. One game gets a player to run over people on the street. Players who do well at this game end up "killing" so many people to score points.

Directions: Pick your favorite videogame. Is it violent in some way? Why do you like this game? Complete the sentences below.

1. My favorite videogame is _____

2. The point of this videogame is to _____

_____

_____

3. I like this videogame best of all because _____

_____

_____

4. This videogame could be violent because _____

_____

_____

5. My feelings about violence in the real world are _____

_____

_____

_____

6. My feelings about violence in videogames are _____

_____

_____

7. I think many people my age like violent videogames because _____

_____

_____

_____

How Do You Feel?

What do you feel in your body when you play videogames? What do you feel in your mind? Many people find that their body and mind change when they play videogames.

Directions: Play a videogame for 10 minutes. This can be at school, at home, or at a friend's house. When you have finished, answer the questions below.

1. What game did you play?

2. What is the goal of this videogame?

3. How did your body change as you played this game? Did your heartbeat change? Did your hands sweat? Did you feel full of energy?

4. How did your mind change when you played this game? Did you start to feel happy? Sad? Tense? Excited?

Play 10 more minutes of this videogame. Watch for changes in your body. Be aware of how your mind changes as you play. Then answer these additional questions.

5. Overall, how did playing this videogame make your body feel? Give at least a one-sentence answer.

6. Overall, how did playing this videogame make your mind feel? Give at least a one-sentence answer.

7. Is this videogame an example of healthy or unhealthy media?

Your Favorite Videogame

Now you can see that videogames are an exciting kind of media, but what do you find when you look closely at one game?

Directions: Pick your favorite videogame. Write a review of it for a gaming magazine. Remember that a review is not just a description of an item. It also gives your thoughts and feelings about an item. In your review, make sure to write about the following:

- brand name and name of videogame
- who will enjoy the game
- what type of world you enter through this game
- how techniques of persuasion are used in this game
- the obvious and hidden messages in this game
- whether you believe this game to be a healthy or unhealthy form of media

Videogame Debate

A debate is an organized discussion. Two people or two groups present two different sides of an issue.

Hold a debate in your classroom so that you can understand your feelings about videogames. You will need encyclopedias and the Internet, sheets of paper, pencils or pens, a stopwatch or clock with a second hand.

Directions: Form two groups. One group will argue the positive side of videogames. This group speaks in support of videogames. The other group will argue the negative side of videogames. This group speaks against them.

Choose one person to be the writer for your group. Look at the topics in the list below. Use encyclopedias and the Internet to find out more about each topic. The writer should take notes on what you have found. For example, if you want to study the link between **videogames** and **homework**, type those words into a search engine or look for them under "videogames" in your encyclopedia. Use the information you find to come up with arguments for or against videogames in each topic. Here is an example.

"My group likes videogames. We found that parents use videogames to help teach their children math and science. This helps kids with homework."

If your group does not like videogames, you might write something like this.

"Children spend three hours a night playing videogames. They do not have time to do their homework."

Spend some time practicing your arguments to get ready for the debate. Once it is time for the debate, ask an adult to be the moderator. Choose one person from each group to be the speaker for the first topic. Pick a group through a coin toss to go first. The moderator calls out a topic. The speaker from the first group has one minute to make an argument. At the end of the minute, the speaker from the second group has a minute to debate the opposite view.

Select another person from your group to speak about the next topic. Now the second group goes first. The speaker has one minute to present his or her views, and so on. Be sure to leave five minutes at the end so that both groups can talk about videogames as a whole. Use the chart on page 79 to make notes during the debate.

Debate Topics

- violence
- relationships with family and friends
- exercise
- effects on body and mind

Videogame Debate *(cont.)*

Directions: Use this page to make notes and record the debate. You do not need to use full sentences. This will help you keep track of arguments from both sides and also help you decide, at the end, which side of the debate you agree with.

For Videogames	Against Videogames

1. Which argument(s) did you agree with? Why? _____

   _____

2. Which argument(s) did you not agree with? Why? _____

   _____

3. Would any of the arguments stop you from playing videogames? Why? _____

   _____

4. Which team do you think presented the best arguments? Why? _____

   _____

Packaging

Boxes, bags, tubes, cartons, cans, and bottles. So many of the items we use every day come in packages. You eat cereal from a box and use a bottle of shampoo. Popcorn and potato chips come in bags. Ice cream comes in a carton. These are all packages, and they are all forms of media.

Long ago, people with something to sell began to wrap their item in paper. They wrote the item's name on the package. People began to sell things in bottles and jars. They pasted a label on the outside. Back then, people made each label by hand. They even made the bottles and jars by hand.

These days we have machines that print thousands of labels at a time. A package gives us clues about the item inside. We use the pictures and words on the package to decide whether we want to buy an item.

Here are a few things that the maker of a package thinks about:

• shape	• brand-name
• color	• slogan
• pictures	• graphics
• writing	• font
• size	

These are all important parts of a package!

Directions: Study the package above and then answer these questions.

1. What item is being sold?

_____

2. What brand name can you find on this package?

_____

3. What slogan is used on this package?

_____

4. What media trick is used on this package?

_____

_____

Packages from the Past

Packages have been around since the 1700s. What did packages from the past look like?

Directions: Study this package label for chocolates, created in 1886. Circle the letter that best completes each sentence.

Image courtesy of the Library of Congress, Prints and Photographs Division (LC-USZ62-92565)

1. The items being sold are

    a. owls.

    b. chefs.

    c. chocolates.

    d. boxes.

2. The brand name on this label is

    a. chocolate.

    b. creams.

    c. pure.

    d. owl.

3. The slogan on this label is

    a. absolutely pure.

    b. owl brand.

    c. chocolate creams.

    d. there is no slogan

4. The clear message on this label is that the chocolate creams are

    a. owls.

    b. pure.

    c. creamy.

    d. expensive.

5. The owl is a symbol of

    a. chocolate.

    b. illness.

    c. candy.

    d. wisdom

Packages of Today

So many items come in packages today. What does the maker of a package want you to see and feel when you look at a box, bag, tube, carton, can, or bottle? Take a close look at one package to find out!

Directions: Pick your favorite package to study. Draw it in the box on the right side of the page. On the left side of the page, answer questions about the package you chose.

1. What is being sold?

   _____

2. What is the brand name on this package?

   _____

3. What is the slogan on this package?

   _____

   _____

4. Who would like this package?

   _____

   _____

5. What obvious message do you see in this package?

   _____

   _____

   _____

6. What hidden message do you see in this package?

   _____

   _____

   _____

7. In what ways is this package a healthy or unhealthy example of media?

   _____

   _____

   _____

Colors, Shapes, and Words

What shape should you make a package for a strange new toy? What color should you make a box for a cell phone? How many words should you put on a bag of peanuts? People who make packages have to ask themselves these kinds of questions every day.

Here are some facts about packages, below.

Package Facts

- Buyers feel calm when they see the color blue.
- The colors red, yellow, and orange make buyers feel hungry.
- The color green makes buyers think of the Earth.
- Buyers find mystery in the color purple.
- Buyers want to buy a product if the package has lots of information on it.
- Buyers like packages in strange shapes.
- Cartoon and superhero characters on packages appeal to kids.

Directions: Study the package facts above, and then answer these questions.

1. What color would you make a box that holds a complicated printer for your computer?

   _____

2. What color would you make a tube that will hold seeds to plant in the garden?

   _____

3. What picture would you put on a bag of mini-donuts for kids?

   _____

4. What color would you make a box that holds a magic wand and a cape?

   _____

5. What color would you make a bag of chocolate-covered raisins?

   _____

6. What shape would you make a package that holds a large three-dimensional puzzle?

   _____

7. What type of information would you put on a package that holds children's vitamins?

   _____

   _____

   _____

Compare and Contrast

How have packages changed over the centuries? Do they have more writing now? Fewer pictures? Which do you prefer?

Directions: Examine the two packages on page 85 and then complete the chart below. Once you have finished, use the information you have learned to write a short essay. In it, point out the differences between packages in the past and packages now. Pay extra attention to words, pictures, brand names, and promises.

Question	Package from the Past	Package from the Present
1. What is being sold?		
2. What is the brand name?		
3. What stands out about the words on this label?		
4. What stands out about the picture on this label?		
5. What does this label promise buyers?		

Image courtesy of the Library of Congress, Prints and Photographs Division (LC-USZ61-1538)

Make Your Own Package

You know now that the makers of packages have to think about words, pictures, slogans, brand names, shapes, and colors. Can you keep these in mind as you design a package of your own?

You will need scratch paper, a pencil with an eraser, one piece of large construction paper, glue or tape, markers or colored pencils, and a ruler.

Directions:

1. Decide what product you are selling with your package. Sketch a picture of your package on scratch paper. Think of a brand name, a slogan, words, pictures, and anything else you think will help to sell the item.

2. Decide on a size, color (or colors), and shape for your package.

3. Make your package out of construction paper. Fold your package into a three-dimensional shape (use the pictures below to help) and glue or tape it.

4. Draw words and pictures, brand names and slogan on your package with markers or colored pencils.

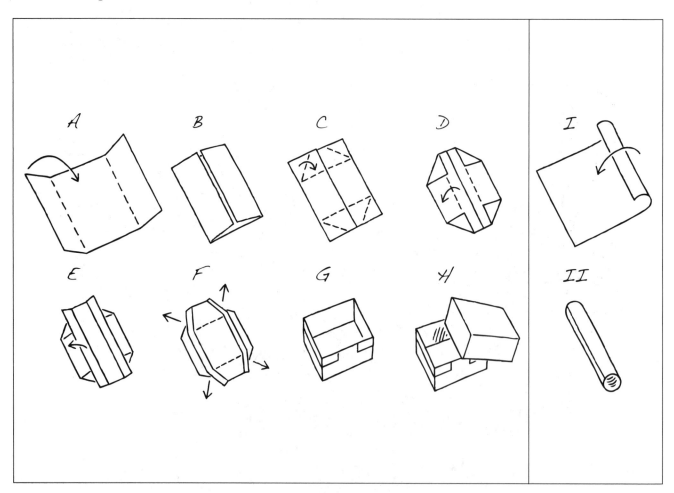

Product Placement

Your favorite television star always wears one kind of watch. The dog on the funny movie plays with one brand of tennis ball. The singer you like sang a song about one type of videogame. These are examples of product placement. Product placement happens when a brand name item appears in a form of media such as on a television program, in a movie, or in a song.

Here are some more examples of product placement.

- A counting book for first-graders uses Snarky's Donuts with numbers in the middle.
- A videogame asks the hero to run around picking up Yum-Yum's chocolate-covered graham crackers.
- The host of a radio show tells the listeners that he is wearing Cool-Soles Sneakers.
- A girl in your favorite movie wears Sweet-Girl shorts and chews Gummy's Bubble Gum.

Product placements are not advertisements. Ads give clear messages: "You need to buy this item." Product placement gives more hidden messages. A product placed in a book, a movie, or a song makes us feel that we will be as happy or attractive as the people using this product.

Products Placed

The seller of an item places a product in a television show or a movie, in a book or on a videogame. The seller hopes that the item will look natural—not like an ad. He or she hopes that people will buy a brand-name item without even knowing that they have seen it in the media!

There are three ways to place a product in media:

1. It just happens. An actor, a director, or a set decorator wants to use a brand name product and just picks one at random without regard for a brand. This makes a movie, a television program, and other forms of media look more real. For example, can you relate more to a character who eats a package of Fudgy-Chunk cookies in one sitting, or to a character who eats treats that you do not recognize?

2. Product placement may be a trade. A movie director will put one brand of sports car in a film. The seller promises to give a sports car to each member of the cast.

3. Someone pays for product placement. The seller of one brand of basketball pays a radio show producer to make sure that the special guest on his show mentions this brand.

Directions: Find and watch a movie preview. You can see these on television, at the movies, or on the Internet. The preview should be no longer than three minutes. You can find hundreds of previews by typing the words *movie trailer* into an Internet search engine.

Make notes while watching the preview writing down every brand name item you see in the movie preview.

Name of movie being previewed _____

Product Placed Within the Preview

1. _____   6. _____

2. _____   7. _____

3. _____   8. _____

4. _____   9. _____

5. _____   10. _____

Products in Books

Sometimes a book for little kids has a name-brand product in it. This is popular for books that teach children how to count and how to read. Children like sweet treats. Sellers like to put candy and cookies into these books. They hope that kids will ask their parents for these items by brand name.

Directions: Study these pages from a children's reading book, and then answer the questions at the bottom of the page.

1. What products are placed in this book?

   _____

2. Who paid for these products to be placed in the book?

   _____

3. Who will like this book?

   _____

   _____

4. What clear messages do you see in this book?

   _____

   _____

5. What hidden messages do you see in this book?

   _____

   _____

6. Is this book an example of healthy or unhealthy media?

   _____

   _____

Products in Videogames

Products started to show up in videogames in the 1980s. One game from 1989 showed boxes from a pizza store. Another game had a cartoon figure from a soft drink. The bananas in one game have stickers with a brand name on them.

Games of today show fast food restaurants. They show brand-name cell phones. They also show candy and soda. Have you noticed any products in the videogames that you play?

Directions: Answer the questions below. This will help you to understand why products are placed in videogames.

1. Why do you think sellers want to put their products in videogames?

   _____

   _____

2. Why do you think the makers of videogames want to put name-brand products in their games?

   _____

   _____

3. Do you think players like product placement in videogames, or dislike them? Explain your answer.

   _____

   _____

4. How do you think players feel when they see brand-name products in their videogames?

   _____

   _____

Now you get to think like someone who makes videogames. Make up a game. In the space below, draw a scene from your game. Add at least three examples of product placement. Make sure to write the name of each brand on your products.

Products on Television

You know from the chapter on television shows that sellers like to place ads for toys and sweet foods in between shows for children. But did you know that they also place their products on the television shows themselves, too?

Directions: Choose a children's television program that is between 30 and 60 minutes in length. Watch the program. See how many name-brand products you can find. Write them down in the space below and explain how they are used. Here is an example of what you might write.

In this television show, Martin wears a Rip-Roar T-shirt and Tank-Tough jeans. He eats a bag of Poppy's Cheese Popcorn and uses a No-Dead-Zone cell phone.

Pay attention to brand-name clothing, shoes, hats, food and drinks, computers and videogames, cell phones, stores, restaurants, sports equipment, and toys.

_____

_____

_____

_____

_____

_____

_____

_____

_____

_____

_____

_____

_____

_____

_____

_____

Taste Test!

Does name brand bottled water taste better than tap water, or do we simply think what sellers tell us to think?

Hold a blind taste test to find out which water you like best. You will need a one liter bottle of name brand bottled water, a one liter bottle of tap water, two brown paper grocery bags, scissors, masking tape, a pen, small paper cups (two for each student), scrap paper (one small piece for each student), and a receptacle for scrap paper (a bowl, hat, or paper bag).

Directions:

1. Ask your teacher to be the tester. Cut bags to fit around each liter bottle. Tape them so you cannot read the labels. On one bottle write *Water #1*. On the second bottle write *Water #2*.

2. All students should line up for a taste test. Everyone but the first student should stay five feet away from the tester. The tester will pour a little water from the first bottle into a cup and the first student will drink it. The tester will then pour a little water from the second bottle for the student to taste.

3. The student will taste both kinds of water then he or she will write down their favorite bottle, number one or number two on a piece of scrap paper. They will fold it and put it in the bowl or bag. Do not talk about your taste test with other students! When the first student is finished, ask the next student to taste both types of water, and so on.

4. When everyone has finished tasting, look at the pieces of paper. Count them to find out which water students liked the best. Then, take the labels off of the water bottles. Discuss the following questions with the rest of your class.

   • Were you surprised by which water the class liked best?

   • What differences did people notice in taste between the two types of water?

   • Why might someone choose to buy name-brand water instead of tap water?

   • Why might someone choose to drink tap water over name-brand water?

   • How do you think product placement affects students?

Products in Movies

You have studied product placement in television shows. You can also study the placement of products in a movie.

Directions: Choose a movie and watch it carefully. Take notes on how many brand-name products you can find mentioned within the movie.

In the space below, write down the products and explain how they are used. Here is an example of what you might write.

In the movie, "Fifth-Grade Mix-Up," Marty and Sam wear Sun-Be-Gone sunscreen. Their parents drive an Aries Flight car. The kids eat at a Pickles' fast food restaurant and they go out for ice cream at Benny's Flavors.

Pay attention to brand-name clothing, shoes, hats, food and drinks, computers and videogames, cell phones, stores, restaurants, sports equipment, and toys.

_____

_____

_____

_____

_____

_____

_____

_____

_____

_____

_____

_____

_____

_____

_____

_____

_____

_____

Magazines

Magazines are a form of media. There are thousands of magazines in print all over the world. Some come out each week. Some come out every month. You can hold some magazines in your hand. You can read some on the Internet.

What is your hobby? Chances are there is a magazine about that hobby. There are cat magazines and dog magazines. There are magazines about cooking and running and surfing. Do you love cars? There is a magazine for you! Like to ride your bike? There are many magazines about bikes.

The first magazines for kids appeared in the 1900s. Today there are still many magazines for kids. Just as in other forms of media, these magazines have symbols, media tricks, messages, and healthy or unhealthy parts to them.

Directions: Study this magazine cover from 1898, and then answer true or false to the statements below.

Image courtesy of The National Archives (533225)

1. The title of the magazine is the biggest writing on the page.

   True   **False**

2. The media trick used by this magazine is symbols.

   True   **False**

3. This magazine is about fashion.

   True   **False**

4. This magazine cover is patriotic.

   True   **False**

5. This magazine cover says that people do not need to help their country.

   True   **False**

Photo Tricks

You wash and brush your dog, but he never looks as pretty as the dog in your favorite magazine. You help your father frost a birthday cake. But even though you put roses on it, it does not look like the cake on the cover of the cooking magazine.

Magazine photographers use all sorts of tricks so that the subject of their photos looks perfect. Here are some of their tricks.

- How do those fried eggs come out in a shiny sunny-side-up on the plate? Photographers sometimes spray a mixture of corn syrup and water on food to make it extra-shiny.

- Why does steam drift up from the pot roast on the cover of the food magazine? Photographers sometimes soak cotton balls in water. Then they put them in the microwave. Finally, they place the heated cotton balls behind the cold pot roast to make it look like it is steaming.

- How does that movie actress in the magazine get such perfect skin and golden blond hair? The girl may have a pimple, but magazine photographers can make it go away on a computer. They can even change someone's dirty blond hair to gold!

- When you see your favorite singer in concert, he is very skinny. On the cover of a magazine that week, he has big muscles. Sometimes magazine photographers use the computer to paste one person's head onto another person's body.

- Did that dog really fit six tennis balls into its mouth as shown in the dog magazine? Maybe, and maybe not. Photographers can use the computer to add extra tennis balls to the dog's mouth!

Photo Tricks (cont.)

Now you see how photographers can change a picture to make it look different from the real subject. Study how these pictures in magazines might make people feel.

Directions: Study each scene below. Circle the letter or letters that best explains how each photo might affect a person:

1. A fifth-grade student looks at a magazine photo of a boy riding a unicycle down a steep hill. He tries the trick and falls down. He

   a. decides never to ride a unicycle again.

   b. feels that he is not a very good athlete.

   c. sells his unicycle and buys a bicycle instead.

   d. does none of the above.

2. An 11-year-old girl wants to make a birdhouse like the one on the cover of her favorite magazine. But her finished birdhouse doesn't look as good. She

   a. throws her birdhouse in the trash.

   b. puts her birdhouse in the yard and feels good knowing she made it herself even if it's not perfect.

   c. takes her birdhouse apart and tries again to make it look like the photo.

   d. does none of the above.

3. Two children see a magazine photo of a pretty garden. They plant flowers and vegetables in neat rows just like the photo. However, bugs eat some of the flowers, and the vegetables come up in strange places. The children

   a. decide they are not very good gardeners.

   b. dig up the plot and start over.

   c. enjoy spending time in the garden anyway.

   d. do none of the above.

4. Students read a magazine in school that shows two thin, good-looking children smiling on the cover in expensive clothes. The students

   a. think that being thin and attractive is important.

   b. want to buy expensive clothes.

   c. know that the photographs have probably been changed on the computer.

   d. do none of the above.

Magazines for Children

You can compare and contrast two magazines for children. This will help you to understand photos, ads, and stories in magazines.

Directions: Choose one magazine from the first list. Choose another magazine from the second list. You can compare these magazines in print form, or you can compare them on the Internet.

List One	List Two
Teen Voices	YM
Skipping Stones	National Geographic Kids
The Writer's Slate	CosmoGirl!
Cat Fancy	Girls' Life
Dog Fancy	Elle Girl
New Moon	Teen Vogue
Cobblestone	American Girl
Boys' Life	Kayak

Now, fill out the chart below.

Question	Magazine One	Magazine Two
1. What is the name of this magazine?		
2. Who will like this magazine?		
3. What are some clear messages in this magazine?		
4. What are some hidden messages in this magazine?		
5. What media tricks do you find in this magazine?		
6. Is this magazine an example of healthy or unhealthy media?		

In the space below or on a separate piece of paper, write a paragraph to compare and contrast these two magazines.

Healthy Messages?

Do magazines for children have healthy messages in their pages? Or do they have unhealthy messages? Can a magazine for children have both kinds of messages?

Directions: Study the magazine covers below and on page 99. Circle the letter that best completes each statement.

1. The title of this magazine mentions your
   a. mind.   b. appearance.   c. kindness.

2. The media trick on this magazine cover is
   a. name-calling.   b. humor.   c. beautiful people.

3. One clear message on this cover says that
   a. this magazine is about style.   c. being popular is important.
   b. this magazine makes kids feel bad about themselves.

4. One hidden message on this cover says that
   a. you should look like a movie star.   c. you should not worry about the way you look.
   b. it is important to be kind to animals.

5. The kids on the cover of this magazine are
   a. athletic.   b. attractive.   c. helpful.

6. This magazine cover may make readers want to improve their
   a. style.   b. brains.   c. photography.

Healthy Messages? *(cont.)*

Directions: Study the magazine cover below. Circle the letter that best completes each sentence.

"You Can Change the World"

Help

5th Graders Adopt a 1st-Grade Reading Class.

One Boy's Story of Helping a Homeless Dog.

Help Your Grandparents! Here's How...

1. The title of this magazine mentions your
   a. kindness.   b. appearance.   c. health.

2. The media trick on this magazine cover is
   a. warm and fuzzy.   b. testimonial.   c. bribery.

3. One clear message on this cover says that
   a. this magazine is about style.   c. you can change the world.
   b. this magazine makes kids feel good about themselves.

4. One hidden message on this cover says that
   a. it is fun to teach kids how to read.   c. you should be popular.
   b. it is important to dress in expensive clothes.

5. The older kid on the cover of this magazine is
   a. bored.   b. fashionable.   c. helpful.

6. This magazine cover may make readers want to
   a. buy clothes.   b. help people and pets.   c. be thin and beautiful.

Your Favorite Magazine

What is your favorite magazine? Do you like to read about cats? Dancing? Beads? Camping?

Directions: Choose your favorite magazine and study it. Answer the questions below in complete sentences and then sketch the cover in the box at the bottom of the page.

1. What is the name of this magazine?

   _____

2. Who will like this magazine?

   _____

3. What media tricks do you see in this magazine?

   _____

4. What are the clear messages in this magazine?

   _____

   _____

5. What are the hidden messages in this magazine?

   _____

   _____

6. Is this magazine a healthy or unhealthy example of media? Why?

   _____

   _____

   _____

Make a Healthy Magazine

What kinds of pictures and words go into a healthy magazine? Make one of your own, and find out! You will need scrap paper and pencils, several sheets of white or colored paper (9" x 11"), markers, stickers, glitter, glue, scissors, a three-hole punch, and three metal brads, or ribbon 2' long.

Directions

- As a class, decide if you want to make a magazine as a class or in groups of three-to-four students. Decide on a group, then, talk about what type of magazine you want to make. Will it be about one topic like pets or sports? Will it be general, with many topics?

- Talk about what pictures and words will make this a healthy form of media. Write down ideas for your magazine on scrap paper.

- Decide who in the group will write stories and who will draw pictures or take photos. Decide on a layout for your magazine. Where will the stories go on each page? Where will the pictures go?

- Create each page of your magazine. You may want to write and draw on each page. Or, you can write stories and draw pictures on separate pieces of paper, then glue them to your magazine pages.

- Use the three-hole punch to carefully punch holes into your magazine pages. Use metal brads to hold the pages together. Or you can weave a ribbon through the holes and tie it in a bow.

- Answer the questions below. Then, pass your magazine around in class for everyone to read!

1. Who will like your magazine?

   _____

2. What media tricks does your magazine use?

   _____

   _____

3. What clear messages are in your magazine?

   _____

   _____

4. What hidden messages are in your magazine?

   _____

   _____

5. How is your magazine a healthy form of media?

   _____

   _____

   _____

Newspapers

"Earthquake Hits Major City!" "Forest Fire Out of Control!" "Stranded Hikers Found Alive!"

Newspapers demand our attention. They have big, bold letters. They have exciting photos. This form of media tells us what is going on in our town, our state, and our world.

Newspapers have been around since the 1400s. They were written by hand. They told stories about people, wars, and money. Newspapers today tell similar stories!

Sometimes these early newspapers tried to be very exciting. Early German papers reported crimes committed in Transylvania by a count named Vlad Tsepes Drakul… otherwise known as Count Dracula!

The first newspaper appeared in America in 1690. It was called *Publick Occurrences*. The government had not approved the publication of this newspaper. The publisher of this paper lived in Boston. He was arrested. The copies of his newspaper were destroyed. But 100 years later there were so many newspapers in the American colonies. Everyone could read about how people wanted freedom from the King of England. These early newspapers inspired people to fight the Revolutionary War!

Thomas Jefferson wrote in 1787, "Were it left to me to decide whether we should have a government without newspapers, or newspapers without a government, I should not hesitate a moment to prefer the latter."

Today we can read thousands of newspapers. They are printed in almost every language found around the world. People can read newspapers that they hold in their hands. They can also read newspapers on the Internet. Some people read both kinds at once!

Front Pages of the Past

Newspapers of today are much different from newspapers of the past. But in some ways, they are the same. You can compare and contrast them by looking at their front pages.

Directions: Study the front page of this newspaper from San Francisco. Fill out the crossword puzzle on the next page.

Image courtesy of the Library of Congress, Prints and Photographs Division (LC-USZ62-73826)

Directions: Study the page from the *Call-Chronicle-Examiner* from 1906 on page 103 and fill in the crossword.

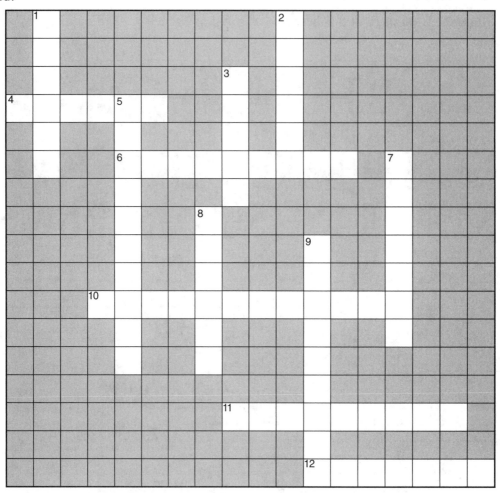

Across

4. The main headline on this front page described the city as this. (6)

6. This U.S. president placed San Francisco under martial law. (9)

10. This newspaper was published in this city.

11. The San Francisco earthquake struck on this day. (9)

12. This was the San Francisco mayor's last name in 1906. (7)

Down

1. The earthquake lasted just under this time frame. (6)

2. On the front page, this is another word for on fire. (1, 5)

3. This was cut off because of the disaster. (5)

5. The main story on this front page is about this. (10)

7. Another word for earthquake is this term in the main story. (7)

8. This newspaper says that natural disasters destroyed this building. (6)

9. John Bermingham, Jr. had to blow this up to stop the fires. (9)

Your Local Paper

Your local newspaper gives a lot of information about your city or town.

Directions: Get a copy of your local newspaper. You can find one at the library or bookstore. You can also get a newspaper from a box on many street corners. Study the newspaper and then answer the questions below. In the space at the bottom, quickly sketch the front page of the newspaper. Make sure you include the name, date, headlines and any images.

1. What is the name of the newspaper?

   _____

2. For how many years has this newspaper been published?

   _____

3. What is its circulation (that is, how many readers does it have)?

   _____

4. Who do you think would like this newspaper?

   _____

5. What stories appear on the front page?

   _____

   _____

6. Which story is the most important? How can you tell?

   _____

   _____

Your Local Paper *(cont.)*

Directions: Now, examine each section of your local newspaper. Write the name of each section on the chart below. Describe it. Explain what types of articles it has. See the example below for details.

Section	Description	Featured Articles
Outdoors	It has stories, calendar events, photos, and interviews.	Story on camping. Story on fishing. Essay and photos on where to see autumn leaves.

The Op/Ed Page

The Op/Ed Page is another term for the Opinion/Editorial Page. What do those words mean? Use a dictionary to look up the word opinion. Write the definition below.

Now use a dictionary to look up the word editorial. Write the definition below.

Newspaper editors write the editorials. People just like you give their opinions in letters to the editor, and in columns.

Look at the Opinion/Editorial page of your paper. It will tell you what the people in your town think and feel about many different things.

Directions: Study the Op/Ed page of your local paper and then answer the questions below.

1. What are the editorials about on this Op/Ed page? List them below.

   _____

   _____

   _____

2. What are the topics of the opinion columns (not the editorials) in the Op/Ed pages?

   _____

   _____

   _____

3. What topics are mentioned in the letters to the editor in the Op/Ed pages? List them below.

   _____

   _____

   _____

   _____

Describe what the Op/Ed pages of your local paper say about the people in your town or city. What do they want? What do they believe?

_____

_____

_____

_____

_____

_____

Write a Letter to the Editor

You can write a letter to the editor of your local newspaper. It might even get published!   The next two pages will show you how to write and send a letter to the editor of your newspaper.

Directions: Think of a topic that you feel strongly about. Maybe you want to write about how homeless people need help. You might want to write about how to help stray cats in your city. Or you might want to write a letter saying "thank you" to someone in your town.

In the space below, write a draft of your letter.

Date: _____

Dear _____ ,

_____

_____

_____

_____

_____

_____

_____

Sincerely,

My Name: _____

Address: _____
Phone: _____
Email: _____

Send a Letter to the Editor

It is easy to send a letter to the editor of your local newspaper. Some editors want you to e-mail your letter. Some want you to send your letter through the post office. Editors get dozens of letters a day. They do not always have the space to publish all letters. Still, they always read them.

Directions: Study the Letters to the Editor page of your local newspaper. Find the directions for how to send your own letter. Below, write down the steps you must take to send your letter to the editor.

Steps for Sending a Letter to the Editor

1. _____
   _____
   _____
   _____

2. _____
   _____
   _____
   _____

3. _____
   _____
   _____
   _____

4. _____
   _____
   _____
   _____

Now, look at your letter to the editor. Check it for correct spelling, punctuation, and grammar. Type your letter on paper or into an e-mail. Ask your teacher or parent to check over your letter. Then, send it to the editor. Follow the steps you wrote above.

Sometimes, an editor will publish a letter the day after it is received. Other times, an editor will hold on to your letter for weeks before publishing it. Keep checking your local paper for your letter!

Comic Strips

Do you read the comics in the newspaper each day? Comic strips first started to appear in newspapers in the early 1900s. One of the first comics was called "The Yellow Kid." The Yellow Kid was a bald child in a yellow nightshirt. He liked to hang around in the alley. People could read "The Yellow Kid" comic strip in the Sunday paper.

Image courtesy of the Library of Congress, Prints and Photographs Division (LC-USZ6-2274)

Directions: Write a paragraph about how "The Yellow Kid" differs from comic strips that appear in the newspaper today. Do you think "The Yellow Kid" would appear in a newspaper today? Why or why not?

_____

_____

_____

_____

_____

_____

_____

_____

_____

Comic Strips *(cont.)*

Now it is your turn to design a healthy newspaper comic strip. Draw your comic strip in the spaces below. Add words. Remember that your comic strip must have the following things.

- characters
- pictures
- words
- symbols

- humor
- name
- media trick

Now, fill in the blank spaces in the essay below to describe your comic strip.

My comic strip is called _____. The main characters are named _____

and _____, and_____.

In my comic strip, _____ is a symbol for _____.

The media trick I use in my comic strip is _____.

What is funny about my comic strip is that _____

_____

_____.

Art

Art is one of the first things that kids do when they are little. Did you draw or paint as a toddler? Maybe you made something out of clay. If so, you made media!

You can study art as a form of media just as you can study ads and books and movies. People have made art for thousands of years. They use their art to send a message to the world. Sometimes that message is clear. Sometimes that message is hidden.

Look at the photograph to the right. Dorothea Lange took this photo in 1936. Dorothea was a famous photographer who took pictures of people during the Great Depression.

The Great Depression happened in the 1930s. Thousands of people lost their homes. They did not have jobs. The people in this photo are victims of a drought. Write the definition of drought in the space below.

Image courtesy of the Library of Congress, Prints and Photographs Division (LC-USF34-T01-001825-C)

Drought = _____

Directions: Study the image above and then answer the questions.

1. Why do you think Dorothea Lange took so many photos of poor people?	
2. What clear message do you see in this photo?	
3. What hidden message do you see in this photo?	
4. Is this a healthy or unhealthy example of media?	

Painting

People painted long before they took photographs. Many painters created pictures of world events. Some painted pictures of wars. Others painted pictures of happy families. Just as in photos, you can study paintings for clear and hidden messages. You can also look at paintings to see what was happening in the world at a particular time.

Directions: Study the painting on page 114. Frederick Remington painted it sometime around 1892. It is called "Indian Scouts Watching Custer's Advance."

Use an encyclopedia or the Internet to answer the questions below.

1. Who was General Custer?

   _____

2. What did Custer want to do with the Indians, who are now called Native Americans?

   _____

   _____

3. What are these two people in the painting looking at?

   _____

4. How do you think these two people feel?

   _____

   _____

5. What is the clear message in Remington's painting?

   _____

   _____

6. What is the hidden message in Remington's painting?

   _____

   _____

7. Is this painting a healthy or unhealthy example of media literacy? Why?

   _____

   _____

   _____

   _____

Image courtesy of Denver Public Library, Western History Collection, Frederic Remington, X-33836

Recent Paintings

How has the subject matter of painting changed since the 1800s? How has it stayed the same?

Directions: Using books, encyclopedias, or the Internet, select a painting made in the last ten years. Sketch it in the space below.

You can read short descriptions of each painting in most museums. They appear on a card next to the paintings. Below, write a short description of the painting you have sketched. Give the artist's name.

Explain what is happening in the painting. Describe the clear message. Describe the hidden message. Share whether you believe this art to be a healthy or unhealthy form of media.

Sculpture

People have made sculptures since prehistoric times. Sculptures are made out of clay and bronze and gold and silver. Some artists even make sculptures out of ice and chocolate!

Mount Rushmore is a large sculpture in the Black Hills of South Dakota. An artist named Gutzon Borglum began this sculpture along with 400 helpers in 1927. It shows the faces of four United States presidents.

Directions: Study the photo of the sculpture below. Answer the questions on a seperate piece of paper.

Photo by Larry Jogerst

1. Use an encyclopedia or the Internet to identify the four presidents in the Mount Rushmore sculpture. List their names.

2. Why do you think these four presidents were chosen to be a part of this sculpture?

3. What might these presidents symbolize in the Mount Rushmore sculpture?

4. What clear message do you see in this sculpture?

5. What hidden message do you see in this sculpture?

6. What media trick is used in this sculpture?

7. Is this sculpture a healthy or unhealthy example of media? Explain your answer.

Image courtesy of the Library of Congress, Prints and Photographs Division

(LC-USZ62-103552)

Sculpture has been around for hundreds of years. This photo was taken in 1914. It shows the famous artist, Alexander Calder, making a sculpture.

The figure to the right is likely a sculpture of Ramses II. It was carved into rock in Egypt.

Both of these sculptures have one thing in common—they represent media!

Create your own sculpture as a form of media. You will need a block of clay (any size or color), a small dish of water, and a craft stick.

Directions: Use your block of clay to make a sculpture. Water will help to mold your clay into a shape. Use the craft stick to create sharp details.

Image courtesy of the Library of Congress, Prints and Photographs Division

(LC-DIG-ppmsca-04476)

Photography

Is a picture worth a thousand words? Photography has been around since the mid-1800s. You can find this form of media everywhere. Photos appear in newspapers and magazines. You can find pictures on billboards, on posters, and in art galleries.

Directions: Study the photo below from 1917. These three women are suffragists. Look up the word "suffrage" in your dictionary. Write the definition here.

Suffrage = _____

What do you think these women are doing?

_____

Image courtesy of the Library of Congress, Prints and Photographs Division (LC-USZ62-75334)

Now match the statements on the right to the answers which best fit them.

1. clear message	a. people who want equality
2. hidden message	b. symbol of freedom to vote
3. who will like the photo	c. bandwagon
4. media trick	d. a woman is voting
5. ballot	e. women should be allowed to vote

Photography *(cont.)*

How is photography used as media today? What messages does it send to people who see it?

Directions: Choose a photo from a magazine or newspaper. Using your chosen image, fill out the chart below.

1. Who took this photograph?	
2. Who will like this photograph?	
3. What clear message can you find in this photograph?	
4. What hidden message can you find in this photograph?	
5. What media trick is used in this photograph?	
6. What symbols can you find in this photograph?	
7. Is this photograph an example of healthy or unhealthy media?	

Comic Books

Up, up, and away! Superman was a character in one of the first comic books. In the 1930s, this form of media took off!

Comic books have colorful pictures. They have exciting words and stories. Kids love to read about superheroes like Wonderwoman, Batman and Robin, and Captain America. What comic books do you like to read?

Image courtesy of The National Archives (595420)

Directions: Study the page from this comic book that was published in 1940. Then, answer the questions.

1. Who are the two superheroes on the cover of this comic book?

   _____

2. What is Robin's other name on this comic book cover?

   _____

3. How much did this comic book cost in 1940?

   _____

4. What images might make you want to read this comic book?

   _____

5. What words might make you want to read this comic book?

   _____

   _____

6. What media tricks do you notice on the cover of this comic book?

   _____

   _____

The first Japanese comic books were called *manga*. They appeared in the 1700s. Manga means "unusual pictures."

Today, many manga have black and white drawings and just a few color pages. They inspire anime. *Anime* is animation that becomes part of a television show or movie.

Directions: Find two comic books. One should be from the United States. One should be from Japan. Study them and then compare and contrast the two books below.

1. Name of comic book and country where it was produced?

    a. _____

    b. _____

2. What story does each comic book tell? Write each story in a few sentences below:

    a. _____

    b. _____

3. What does the art look like in each comic book. Is it in color or black and white? How are people and animals shown? Are the drawings simple or complicated?

    a. _____

    b. _____

4. What is the clear message in each comic book?

    a. _____

    b. _____

5. What is the same about these two comic books?

    a. _____

    b. _____

6. How are these two comic books different?

    a. _____

    b. _____

Murals and Graffiti

A mural is a large painting on the side of a building or on a wall. Often, the artist has asked for permission to paint his or her mural.

Graffiti can be one small painting. It can also be very large. Like murals, graffiti appears on the sides of buildings or on walls. But often, the artist has not asked for permission to paint graffiti.

Murals and graffiti are both forms of media. You can study them for clear and hidden messages. Sometimes they use symbols. Often, they use media tricks.

Directions: Study the images below and then, on a separate piece of paper, write out the sentences 1–4 for each image, filling in the blanks to complete them.

1. This is a picture of _____.

2. The technique of persuasion used in this image is _____.

3. The obvious message of this media is _____.

4. The artist may have made this picture to _____.

Finally, write a paragraph to answer the question below.

Why do you think that murals often get good attention, while graffiti often gets bad attention? Explain

your answer. _____

_____

_____

_____

_____

_____

Make a Mural

You can make a mural for your classroom! You will need scratch paper, butcher paper (enough to cover one classroom bulletin board), pencils with erasers, paintbrushes (both thick and thin, one for each person), cans of water-based paint in many colors, newspaper, cleanup rags, and water.

Directions

1. Cover a bulletin board with butcher paper. Tape or staple the paper to the back of the board.

2. Decide as a group what your mural will look like. You might want to make it as a class. Or break into groups of four and sketch a small section of the mural on your own. Draw your designs with a pencil on scratch paper.

3. Get ready to paint! Gather rags and water for cleaning up. Spread newspaper below the wall so you don't get paint on the floor. Outline your mural idea with small brushes and paint. Then, fill in the outlines with paint.

4. Allow the paint to dry and wash the brushes well.

5. Finally, answer the questions below.

1. Who will like your mural?	
2. What clear messages are in your mural?	
3. What hidden messages are in your mural?	
4. What media tricks do you use in your mural?	
5. What symbols do you use in your mural?	
6. Is your mural a healthy or unhealthy example of media?	

Websites

Turn on your computer, connect to the Internet, and the first thing you see is a website. Websites are a complex form of media. They give us so much information through photos, words, ads, and sound.

Media literate kids know to ask these questions whenever they see a website:

- Who made this website?
- What is being sold to me?
- How does this website make me feel?
- What does this website make me want to do?

Directions: Study the website below and then answer the questions.

1. Who will like this website?

   _____

2. How many ads do you count on this website?

   _____

3. Why do you think this photo was chosen for this website?

   _____

   _____

4. What clear messages do you find on this website?

   _____

   _____

5. What hidden messages do you find on this website?

   _____

   _____

6. What media tricks are used on this website?

   _____

   _____

Home Pages

A home page is the main page of a website. It is usually the first page that comes up when you type in the address for a website. A home page gives people an introduction to the rest of the website. It can include photos, words, music, and ads.

There are home pages for every subject you can think of. Do you like to jump rope? There is a home page for you. Do you like to build model planes? Many home pages will show you how.

Directions: Connect to the Internet. Chose one home page to study. If you are not sure which home page to use, try this: In your favorite internet search engine, type in the words *home page* and a subject such as *basketball* or *flowers* or *movie stars*. Ask an adult to help you find the best home page for your research. Study the home page and sketch it in the space below. Then fill in the blanks to create your report. Finally, read your report out loud to your class.

Hello! I am here today to talk about the home page
called _____. It's a very _____
home page that will appeal to who are _____ years old.
The creator of this home page used a few methods of
advertising. These include _____,
_____, and_____. I can
tell that the obvious messages on this home page tell
visitors to _____ and to _____.
But look carefully! You will also find hidden messages
that tell visitors to _____ and _____.
Study this home page for yourself. I think you will find
it a _____ form of media.

Websites for Kids

You will find hundreds of websites for kids on the Internet. There are websites about child movie stars and singers. There are websites for kids who do great things to help other people or animals. Some websites will tell you how to build a birdhouse. Others will tell you how to make an apple pie.

When you look at a website for kids, don't forget to ask yourself these questions.

- Who made this website?
- What is being sold to me?
- How does this website make me feel?
- What does this website make me want to do?

Directions: Search for a kids' website based on the list below. Type the word "kids" into your favorite search engine. Type the name of the topic that interests you. Click on search and ask an adult to help you choose the best site for your research. Then, fill out the chart below.

• history	• science	• books
• nature	• sports	• music
• math	• games	• movies
• animals	• art	• celebrities

1. What is the name of this website?	
2. Who will like this website?	
3. Who made this website?	
4. What is being sold to me on this website?	
5. How does this website make me feel?	
6. What does this website make me want to do?	

Author Websites

What is your favorite book? Who is your favorite author? Many living authors have a website.
They use the Internet to post photos of themselves for kids to see. They also put up interviews and
information on new books. They even post calendars to let readers know the next time they will be in
town to give a reading from their book.

Directions: Choose your favorite author. Locate his or her website with the help of your favorite search
engine. The key words should include the author's name and the words home page. Below, write a
letter to your author. Write about his or her website. Your letter should address the following things.

- Who will like this website
- What is being sold
- How this website makes you feel
- What this website makes you want to do

- Clear and hidden messages on the website
- Media tricks on the website
- Whether this website is healthy or unhealthy media

Date: _____

Dear _____ ,

_____

_____

_____

_____

_____

_____

Sincerely,

My Name: _____

Address: _____

Phone: _____

Email: _____

Podcasts

What is a podcast? It is a program that you can download on your computer. Then you can listen to it on your headphones. A podcast can be news. It can be music. It can be a book or a class or a show.

There are many podcasts made for kids. One of the most popular types is a music podcast. This kind of podcast will include songs and interviews with musicians.

Directions: Download and listen to a podcast about kids' music. Log onto the Internet and link to your favorite search engine. Type in the key words *kids music podcast*. Ask an adult to help you choose a good podcast for your research.

Listen carefully to your chosen podcast. Then, write a two-minute review of this music podcast. Use the example below to help write your review. Pay attention to the following items.

- the name of the podcast
- the host's name
- special guests
- who helped to pay for this podcast
- who will enjoy this podcast

- media tricks used in this podcast
- clear and hidden messages in the podcast
- whether this podcast is healthy or unhealthy

Sample Podcast Review

The podcast *Fifth-Grade Dance Party* will make you kick up your heels and dance! D.J. Solo has a rocking beat and lots of cool guests. Today, 12-year-old country-western superstar JoJo James played her new song, *My Horse is Blue*. Wow, her voice is pretty. She said everyone should own a horse. D.J. Solo used a funny sound effect on the podcast. It sounded like a bugle, and it made me want to run out and buy a horse!

Once you have written your review, record it to make your own podcast.

First read your review aloud once to rehearse. Then read it and record it on your computer as a sound file.

If you need information on how to make a podcast, type the words *record a podcast* into your favorite search engine for step-by-step instructions.

When your podcast is finished, play it for everyone to hear!

Build a Website

Learn how people make websites by building one of your own. Choose a topic as a class and then add pictures, images, short reports, and other fun information to teach other people about your topic. You will need scratch paper, pencils with erasers, and a computer.

You can make your website as a class but this activity is best completed in groups of 3–4. You can simply design a website on paper, or take this project one step further and build it on the computer.

Directions:

1. First you need to decide how many pages you want your website to include. Make sure you include a home page and at least one more page. On scratch paper, sketch a design for your website pages. Decide whether you will include ads and photos. You may want to ask different people in your group to sketch different web pages for your website.

2. Write the words and sketch pictures for your website on the scratch paper. See the illustration for an example.

3. You may choose to build this website on a computer. There are many sites that allow you to build a site for free. They use a template that is easy to follow. To find a site, type the keywords *free website for kids* into your favorite search engine.

4. Follow the computer instructions to build your website. Type in your writing and upload photos. You may want to scan your artwork and upload it, too. Note that it is illegal to upload someone else's writing and pictures from the Internet without getting their permission first.

5. Ask your teacher to review your website. After he or she has given you permission, give your friends and family the link to your website so that they may see it, too!

6. Finally, fill in the blanks to describe your website.

My website will sell _____. It will make kids feel _____. It will make them want to _____.
I have a clear message on my website. It is _____.
I also have a hidden message on my website. It is _____.
I use these media tricks on my _____ website and
I think you will find my website to be a _____ form
of media.

Final Project

Congratulations! You have almost finished your study of Media Literacy. Before you go, show that you have become media literate. Make a final example of media and then write a paper to explain what you have done.

Directions: Choose a project to make from the list below, then, write about it in a one-page essay. Describe the media that you have made. Use all of the terms from this book as you write about your media. Here they are:

- audience
- clear messages
- hidden messages
- media tricks
- healthy or unhealthy media
- symbols

Forms of Media

- billboard
- comic book
- magazine
- newspaper
- package
- painting
- photograph
- podcast
- print ad
- radio ad
- recorded song
- sculpture
- television commercial
- website

_____

_____

_____

_____

_____

_____

_____

_____

_____

_____

Certificate

This is to certify that

_____

has become a media-literate consumer,
skilled in the analysis of:

- Advertisements
- Art
- Magazines
- Movies
- Music
- Newspapers
- Packaging
- Product Placement
- Radio
- Television
- Videogames
- Websites

Signed this _____ of _____.

_____
Teacher's Signature

Answer Key

Page 10 — How Much Media?

Students chart the type of media they are exposed to, along with the amount each day. Grade for thoughtfulness and effort.

Page 11 — Why Does Media Matter?

Students list their favorite form of media along with how it makes them feel. Grade for thoughtfulness and effort.

Page 14 — Slogans and Jingles

Students write a favorite slogan and jingle.

Page 15 — Messages in Media

1. Clear message: wear Sassy Girl blue jeans.

    Hidden message: you will be pretty and popular and get good grades if you wear Sassy Girl blue jeans.

2 Clear message: Eat Quick-Fix hamburgers.

    Hidden message: Hamburgers may not be healthy, but they are desirable.

Page 16 — Propaganda

1. b

2. a

3. c

Page 17 — Find Propaganda

Grade for effort and understanding of propaganda.

Page 18 — Stereotypes

1. Both the star and his sidekick are stereotyped.

Short overweight males might feel that they are less successful. Tall handsome males might feel pressure to succeed.

2. Both girls are stereotyped.

Poor kids might feel that they will never be popular or happy. Rich kids might feel pressured to be happy and popular.

Page 19 — Stereotype or Original?

Grade for effort, creativity, and understanding of stereotyped and original characters.

Page 20 — Healthy Media

1 False
2. True
3. False
4. True

Page 21 — Healthy Media *(cont.)*

1. bicycles
2. slogan
3. fear
4. unhealthy

Grade posters for effort and student understanding of healthy and unhealthy media.

Page 22 — First Media

Grade for effort and creativity.

Page 23 — More on Petroglyphs

Grade for effort and understanding of petroglyphs as media.

Page 24 — Make a Petroglyph

Grade for effort and creativity, as well as for understanding of symbols.

Page 25 — Print Ads

1. c
2. d
3. a

Page 26 — Early Print Ads

1. False
2. True
3. True
4. False
5. True

Page 27 — Early Print Ads *(cont.)*

1. This is an ad for a home washer.
2. This ad will appeal mostly to women.
3. The clear message of this ad is "buy this home washer."
4. The stereotype in this ad suggests that women do all the washing at home.

Page 29 — Print Ads of Today *(cont.)*

Grade for effort and depth of analysis.

Answer Key (cont.)

Page 30 — Same and Different

Grade for effort and understanding of how print ads have changed and/or remained similar over time.

Page 31 — Make Your Own Print Ad

Grade student's own print ad as a form of media for effort, creativity, and understanding.

Page 32 — Billboards

There are at least six products advertised in this photo.

Page 33 — Early Billboards

1. d
2. e
3. c
4. a
5. b

Page 34 — Idea Billboards

The Lions' Club is an international service organization that helps communities and people in need.

1. False
2. False
3. True
4. True

Page 35 — Political Billboards

1. Republican
2. vote for Gerald R. Ford
3. Gerald R. Ford, Jr. to work for you in Congress.
4. Republican voters
5. open to student interpretation. Billboard might imply that Ford's opponents will not work for voters.

Page 36 — Billboards of Today

Grade for effort and depth of analysis.

Page 38 — Compare and Contrast *(cont.)*

Grade for effort and understanding of how billboards have changed over time.

Page 39 — Make Your Own Billboard

Grade for effort and understanding of own billboard as a form of media.

Page 41 — Radio Ads

1. Completed

2. Fear—use suspenseful music, screaming, windows breaking

3. Beautiful people—use actors with sultry, elegant voices

4. Symbols—patriotic music, recognizable tunes like Richard Wagner's "Bridal Chorus," alarm clocks roosters crowing to symbolize morning, crickets to symbolize night, etc.

5. Humor—particularly high- or low-pitched voices, yodeling, tongue-twisters, funny squeaks or slide-whistles, goats bleating, etc.

6. Repetition—repeat a song, a brand name, or a slogan

7. Facts—use a British actor to present evidence in a formal, elegant tone. Have machinery sounds in the background and many big words.

Page 42 — Old Time Radio Ads

Grade for effort and student understanding of radio ads from the past.

Page 43 — Radio Ads of Today

Grade for effort and student understanding of radio ads of the present.

Page 44 — Record a Radio Ad

Grade for effort and student understanding of own radio ad as a form of media.

Pages 45–46 — Old Time Radio Shows

Grade for student understanding of radio shows from the past.

Page 47 — War of the Worlds

1. A narrator introduces the story, and then a radio newscast begins. Music plays, and is abruptly interrupted by the announcer saying that Martians have landed on Earth.

2. People who didn't catch the introduction to this radio piece, and who tuned in only to the simulated broadcast with its reports of Martians landing and scientists confirming this, truly believed Martians had landed on Earth.

3. This is open to students' interpretation. Look for reasonable, thoughtful answers.

Page 48 — Radio Shows for Children

Grade for effort and depth of student analysis.

Page 49 — Record Your Radio Show

Grade for effort and student understanding of own radio show as a form of media.

Page 51 — Your Television Log

Grade for effort and level of details.

Page 52 — Television Ads

Grade for effort and ability to analyze television ads as media.

Answer Key *(cont.)*

Page 53 — Television Ads from the Past

Grade for effort and ability to analyze a television ad from the past.

Page 54 — Television Ads of Today

Grade for effort and ability to analyze a television ad from the present.

Page 56 — Compare and Contrast *(cont.)*

Grade for effort and understanding of how television ads have changed over time.

Page 57 — Make a Television Ad

Grade for effort and understanding of students' own ad as a form of media.

Page 58 — Television News

Grade for effort and understanding of segments of television news.

Page 59 — Healthy or Unhealthy?

Grade for effort and understanding of television news segments as healthy/unhealthy.

Page 60 — Television Advertisers

Grade for effort and understanding of commercials during television programs.

Page 61 — Messages—Clear and Hidden

Grade for effort and understanding of clear and hidden messages in television programs.

Page 62 — The Big Turnoff

Grade for effort and student understanding of one TV Turnoff website.

Page 63 — No TV? No Worries!

Grade for effort and level of detail.

Page 64 — TV Turnoff Week Journal

Grade for effort and level of detail and creativity.

Page 65 — Music

Grade for effort and level of detail.

Page 66 — Problems in Music

Grade for effort and student understanding of one controversial issue in music.

Page 67 — What Is This Song About?

Grade for effort and student understanding of song as a form of media.

Page 68 — Music Videos

Grade for effort and understanding.

Page 69 — Music Videos *(cont.)*

1. Kids would like this video.

2. Student answers will vary. They may say beautiful people, warm and fuzzy, or bandwagon.

3. The clear message is never to give up.

4. The hidden message is that sometimes we need people to help us accomplish a seemingly impossible task.

5. Someone would likely feel happy and inspired after watching this video.

6. This video is a healthy example of media.

Page 70 — More on Music Videos

Grade for effort and student understanding of chosen video as a form of media.

Page 71 — Make a Music Video

Grade for effort and student ability to recognize own music video as a form of video.

Page 72 — Videogames

1. The older joystick is heavier, larger, and boxier. The newer one is more streamlined, less complicated, and the controls look like little spaceships.

2–5. Grade for effort and detail.

Page 73 — Videogame Ads

1. Black Belt Bonanza.

2. Fungamz

3. See, Play, Be

4. Fear

5. Play this videogame.

6. You must beat your opponent in a fierce karate match or you will cry.

7. Student interpretations will differ.

Page 74 — Videogame Ads *(cont.)*

Grade for effort and student understanding of a videogame as a form of media.

Page 75 — Violent Videogames

Grade for effort and understanding of violence in videogames.

Page 76 — How Do You Feel?

Grade for effort and level of detail to physical and emotional changes.

Page 77 — Your Favorite Videogame

Grade for effort and understanding of student's favorite videogame as a form of media.

Page 78 — Videogame Debate

Grade each group for effort and attention to research and detail when formulating arguments for debate.

Answer Key _(cont.)

Page 79 — Videogame Debate *(cont.)*

Grade for effort and understanding of the issues presented.

Page 80 — Packaging

1. grape juice
2. Squeezie's
3. fresh squeezed for your health
4. beautiful people

Page 81 — Packages from the Past

1. c
2. d
3. a
4. b
5. d

Page 82 — Packages of Today

Grade for effort and student understanding of packages as a form of media.

Page 83 — Colors, Shapes, and Words

1. blue
2. green
3. a cartoon character or superhero
4. purple
5. red, orange, or yellow
6. students should indicate some type of innovative package
7. recommended dosage, flavor, slogan, brand-name, facts and possible doctor testimonials

Page 84 — Compare and Contrast

1. a. soap
   b. soap
2. a. Pure White Rock
   b. Suds-Bucket's Laundry Soap
3. a. The words are in various fonts. The center words are large and dramatic.
   b. The text is flashy. Some of it is in bubbles.
4. a. There is a large blue cross in the middle of the label.
   b. There are lots of bubbles.
5. a. The label promises that one package will make a barrel of 10–20 pounds of beautiful white soap.
   b. The label promises that this soap will do the scrubbing for you.

Page 86 — Make Your Own Package

Grade for effort and understanding of student's own package as a form of media.

Page 88 — Products Placed

Grade for effort and student understanding of product placement in a movie trailer.

Page 89 — Products Placed in Books

1. Salties' Corn Chips, Fullo' Nuts Cookies
2. The sellers of these products paid for these items to be placed in books.
3. Kids who are learning to read will like these books.
4. The clear message is to read "boy" and "girl."
5. The hidden message is to buy these products.
6. Student opinions will differ. Likely they will say that this book is unhealthy because corn chips and cookies are not good for kids.

Page 90 — Products Placed in Videogames

Grade for effort and understanding of product placement in videogames.

Page 91 — Products Placed on Television

Grade for effort and understanding of product placement in a television program.

Page 92 — Taste Test!

Grade students for behavior and organization during the taste test.

Page 93 — Products Placed in Movies

Grade for effort and understanding of product placement in a movie.

Page 94 — Magazines

1. true
2. true
3. false
4. true
5. false

Page 96 — Photo Tricks *(cont.)*

1–4. Give credit for any answer since each student will have different opinions.

Page 97 — Magazines for Children

Grade for effort and understanding of children's magazines as a form of media.

Answer Key *(cont.)*

Page 98 — Healthy Messages?

1. b
2. c
3. c
4. a
5. b
6. a

Page 99 — Healthy Messages? *(cont.)*

1. a
2. a
3. c
4. a
5. c
6. b

Page 100 — Your Favorite Magazine

Grade for effort and understanding of a favorite magazine as a form of media.

Page 101 — Make a Healthy Magazine

Grade for effort and understanding of student magazine as a form of media.

Page 104 — Front Pages of the Past *(cont.)*

ACROSS

4. Ruined
6. Roosevelt
10. San Francisco
11. Wednesday
12. Schmitz

DOWN

1. Minute
2. Ablaze
3. Water
5. Earthquake
7. Temblor
8. Church
9. Buildings

Page 105 — Your Local Paper

Grade for effort and level of detail about local paper.

Answer Key (cont.)

Page 106 — Your Local Paper *(cont.)*

Grade for depth and effort.

Page 107 — The Op/Ed Page

Opinion: A view or belief.

Editorial: A newspaper article presenting a belief of the editor or publisher.

Grade for effort and level of detail about op/ed page.

Page 108 — Write a Letter to the Editor

Grade for effort and understanding of how to write a letter to the editor.

Page 109 — Send a Letter to the Editor

Grade for effort and level of detail in explanation of how to send a letter to a local newspaper editor.

Page 110 — Newspaper Comic Strips

Grade for effort and understanding of comic strips of the past and present.

Page 111 — Newspaper Comic Strips *(cont.)*

Grade for effort and understanding of student's own comic strip as a form of media.

Page 112 — Art

Drought = The scarcity of water, sometimes resulting in a loss of crops and homes.

1. Dorothea Lange wanted to show the rest of the world how poor people were affected by drought and by the Depression.
2. The clear message in this photo is that these people are poor and living in harsh conditions.
3. The hidden message in this photo is that those more fortunate should help those left destitute by the Depression.
4. Student opinions may differ. They may say that this photo is frightening, and therefore unhealthy. Most will say that if it raises public awareness of the subjects' plight, then it is a healthy form of media.

Page 113 — Painting

1. General George Armstrong Custer was a U.S. soldier in the Civil War and Indian wars. He led numerous attacks on Native Americans in pursuit of their land.
2. Custer wanted to remove the Indians from their homeland and put them on reservations.
3. These people are probably looking at U.S. soldiers who are coming to fight them and take their land.
4. These people probably feel scared, angry, and anxious.
5. The clear messages is that these two people are watching something.
6. The hidden message varies. Students may say that the picture says that Native Americans were hostile. They may also say that the hidden message is that the U.S. soldiers took advantage of Native Americans and stole their land.
7. Opinions will vary. Students may say that this picture is healthy because it gives a sense of history, or a sense of the Native Americans' plight. They may say that it is unhealthy because it makes Native Americans look warlike.

Answer Key (cont.)

Page 115 — Recent Paintings

Grade for effort and student understanding of painting as a form of media.

Page 116 — Sculpture

1. Washington, Jefferson, Roosevelt, and Lincoln.

2. These four presidents were particularly important in the history of the U.S.

3. These presidents might symbolize power, freedom, and independence from tyranny.

4. The clear message is that there are four U.S. presidents carved into Mount Rushmore.

5. The hidden messages are that these four presidents were particularly important in U.S. history, and that their influence is indestructible like this mountain.

6. The media trick is symbolism.

7. Most students will say that Mount Rushmore is a healthy form of media because it teaches us something about history and symbolizes freedom.

Page 117 — Sculpture *(cont.)*

Grade for effort and understanding of student's sculpture as a form of media.

Page 118 — Suffrage

Suffrage = the right to vote. These women are putting ballots into a ballot box.

1. d

2. e

3. a

4. c

5. b

Page 119 — Photography *(cont.)*

Grade for effort and understanding of photo as a form of media.

Page 120 — Comic Books

1. Batman and Robin appear on this comic book cover.

2. Robin is also called "The Boy Wonder."

3. This comic book cost ten cents in 1940.

4. Students will likely say that the images of the superheroes would make them want to read this book, along with the bat logo at the top of the page.

5. Students will likely say that the words "the brand new adventures of" would make them want to read this comic book.

6. Possible media tricks include beautiful people and hyperbole.

Page 121 — Comic Books *(cont.)*

Grade for effort and thoughtful comparison of two contemporary comic books.

Page 122 — Murals and Graffiti

Grade answers on understanding and effort.

Answer Key *(cont.)*

Page 123 — Make a Mural

Grade for effort and understanding of students' own mural as a form of media.

Page 124 — Websites

1. Kids will like this website.

2. There are at least six ads.

3. This photo was chosen because this website is a kids' search engine, and the kids in this photo are happily studying.

4. The clear messages are that Search-a-lot is for kids, and that research is fun.

5. The hidden messages are that you will be happy if you study, that you should consume the products that are advertised, and that it is good to be smart.

6. The media tricks are symbols and beautiful people.

Page 125 — Home Pages

Grade for effort and understanding of home page as a form of media.

Page 126 — Websites for Kids

Grade for effort and understanding of kids' website as a form of media.

Page 127 — Author Websites

Grade for effort, punctuation and spelling, and understanding of kids' author's website as a form of media.

Page 128 — Podcasts

Grade for effort and creativity, as well as for understanding of podcast as a form of media.

Page 129 — Build a Website

Grade for effort and creativity, as well as for understanding of student's website as a form of media.

Page 130 — Final Project

Grade for effort and creativity, as well as for understanding of student's final project as a form of media.

Resources

For Further Study

Books

Andersen, Neil. *At the Controls: Questioning Video and Computer Games.* Fact Finders, 2007.

Baker, Frank W. *Coming Distractions: Questioning Movies.* Capstone Press, 2007.

Baran, Stanley J. *Introduction to Mass Communication: Media Literacy and Culture.* McGraw-Hill, 2003.

Botzakis, Stergios. *Pretty in Pink: Questioning Magazines.* Fact Finders, 2007.

Silverblatt, Art. *Media Literacy: Keys to Interpreting Media Messages.* Praeger, 2001.

Wan, Guofang. *TV Takeover: Questioning Television.* Fact Finders, 2007.

Organizations

Center for Media Literacy	http://www.medialit.org/
Media Education Foundation	http://www.mediaed.org/
New Mexico Media Literacy Project	http://www.nmmlp.org/
Northwest Media Literacy Center	http://www.mediathink.org/

Websites

General portal for media literacy education	http://www1.medialiteracy.com/
Media literacy clearinghouse	http://www.frankwbaker.com/
Tools for teaching media literacy	http://www.mediachannel.org/classroom/
Media activism site	http://www.mediawatch.com/